Nebraska

AMERICA THE BEAUTIFUL
second series

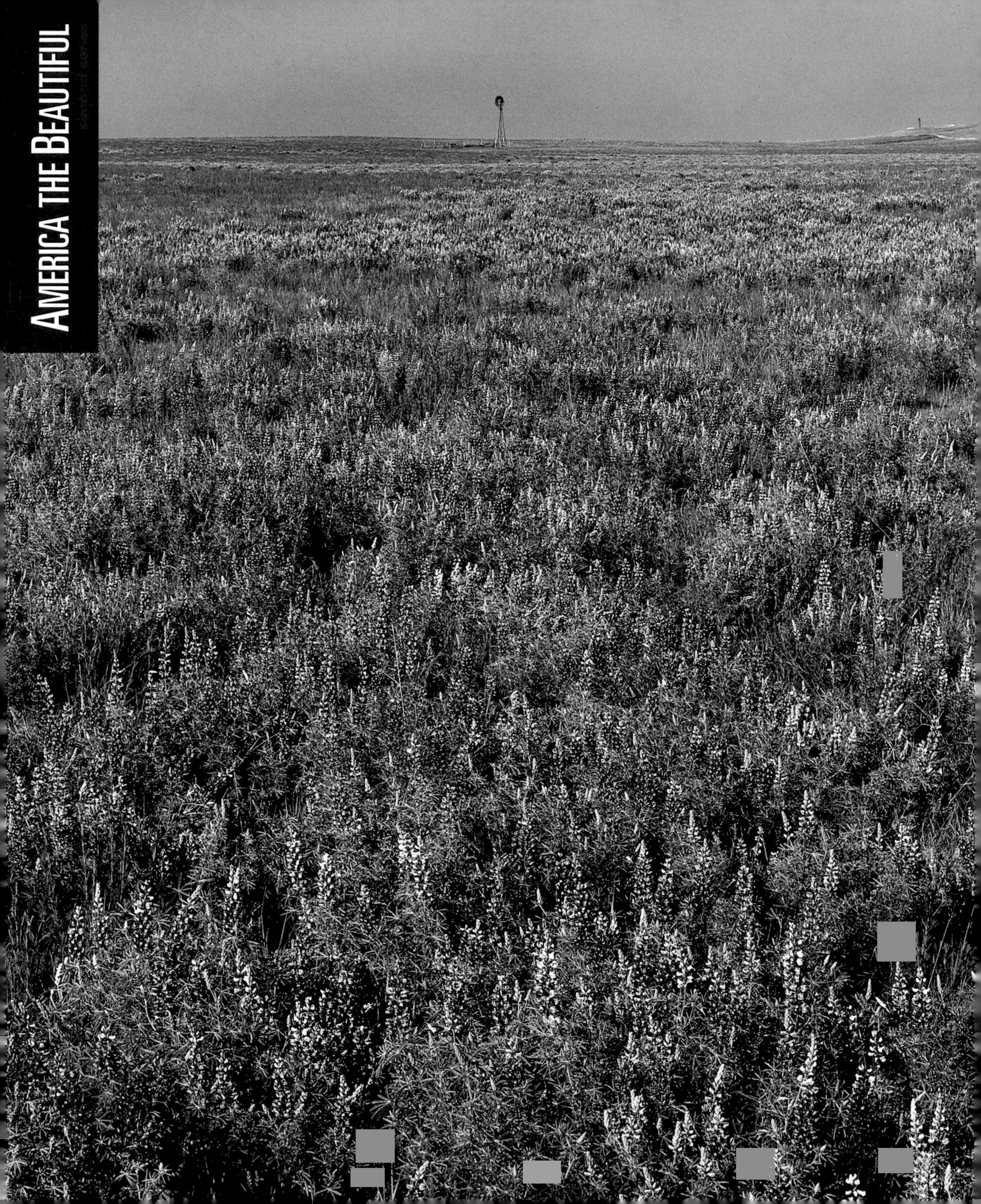

Nebraska

Sylvia McNair

Children's Press®
A Division of Grolier Publishing
New York   London   Hong Kong   Sydney
Danbury, Connecticut

Frontispiece: Nebraska's grasslands

Front cover: Chimney Rock

Back cover: Omaha skyline

Consultant: Jim Potter, State Historian's Office, Nebraska State Historical Society

Please note: All statistics are as up-to-date as possible at the time of publication.

Visit Children's Press on the Internet at http://publishing.grolier.com

Book production by Editorial Directions, Inc.

Library of Congress Cataloging-in-Publication Data

McNair, Sylvia.
    Nebraska / by Sylvia McNair.
      144 p. 24 cm. — (America the beautiful. Second series)
    Includes bibliographical references and index.
    Summary : Describes the geography, ecology, history, economy, religions, culture,
and people of the state of Nebraska.
    ISBN 0-516-20689-3
    1. Nebraska—Juvenile literature. I. Title. II. Series.
F666.3.M39 1999
978.2—dc21   97-40704
                                                                             CIP
                                                                             AC

Acknowledgments

Many people helped in the preparation of this book, and the author is grateful to all of them. Carolyn Wells, of Lisco, Nebraska, shared her firsthand knowledge of life on a Sandhills ranch. She read the manuscript and made many excellent suggestions. Mary Ethel Emanuel of the Nebraska Tourism Office was involved from the beginning, suggesting sources, sharing stories, and reading the manuscript. Both of these women prevented several errors from getting into print, and any errors that remain are the responsibility of the writer. Also helpful in on-the-spot research were Sandra Wikowicz, Tim McNeil, Joni Vaughn, and Nelda Pake. Anna Idol, as usual, helped in the final polishing of the manuscript.

This book is dedicated to all of these people.

Soybean fields

Oregon Trail wagon train

The Omaha skyline

Contents

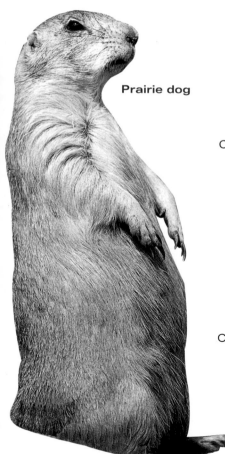

Prairie dog

Chimney Rock

Cattle roundup

Winnebago Powwow

Meadowlark

CHAPTER ONE

Trails, Rails, and Interstates

Settlers camping along the Oregon Trail

"On Monday the 14th of May 1804, we ... proceeded up the Missouri on our intended voyage of discovery," Private Patrick Gass wrote in his journal. He was a member of a group of men who traveled from near St. Louis, Missouri, to the Pacific coast of Oregon and back. The journey took more than two years.

In July, the expedition reached what is now Nebraska. They passed the mouth of the Platte River and continued up the Missouri, spending two months along the present-day east and northeast borders of the state. They saw prairies, woodlands, and occasional high bluffs along the river. They found "a Great Quantity of wild Cherrys," as well as apples, grapes, currants, raspberries, gooseberries, hazelnuts, "and a great variety of Plants & flours [sic] not common to the U.S." They encountered many kinds of wildlife, including two they had not known of before: prairie dogs and antelopes. They had peaceful meetings with delegations of the Oto and Missouri native tribes.

Gass and more than forty other men were under the leadership of Captains Meriwether Lewis and William Clark. The territory they were to explore, mostly by boat, had just become a part of the United States. President Thomas Jefferson had bought it from France through an agreement called the Louisiana Purchase. The men were under orders to keep journals and write descriptions of

Opposite: The Missouri River along the Lewis and Clark National Historic Trail

what they saw as they traveled. The president was especially interested in their observations about geography, science, and transportation routes. They were also instructed to make friends with native tribes.

The men of the Lewis and Clark Expedition were not the first people of European descent to explore the American West, but they were the first to leave a complete account of what they saw.

The Oregon Trail

The first covered wagons began cutting deep ruts along a route called the Oregon Trail in 1830. The trail started at the Mississippi River in Missouri and extended all the way to the Pacific Coast. In present-day Nebraska, much of the route followed the Platte River and its two branches.

By the 1840s, thousands of emigrants were on their way west, their possessions and supplies loaded on ox-drawn wagons. Groups traveled together. A few people rode horseback; most of them walked. Very small children were carried in the wagons, along with elderly and sick people. Many of these pioneers described what they saw in journals or in long letters to their families back home.

Wagons often broke down, and repairs were made with whatever materials could be found. Sicknesses—measles, mountain fever, colds, eye infections, cholera—were some of the hardships the pioneers faced. A missionary who traveled west in 1835 described the torment his horses endured from horseflies. The "bite is like the thrust of the point of a lance, and when the fly is surfeited, or brushed off, the blood immediately gushes out."

The herds of buffalo, or bison, amazed the travelers. "We could

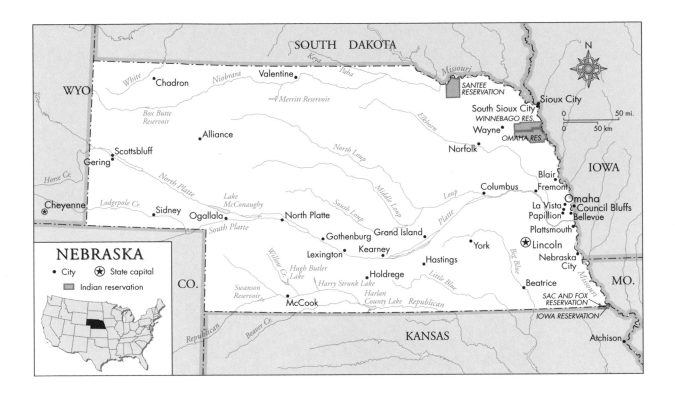

Geopolitical map of
Nebraska

see five thousand head [of buffalo] at once in lots of places," one pioneer wrote. "Where is the limit of their feeding range?" wondered another.

The trail was scorchingly hot in summer, dangerously cold and stormy in winter. A woman wrote in 1853 about a dreadful storm of rain, hail, and lightning: "It killed two oxen. . . .The wind was so high I thought it would tear the wagons to pieces. . . . [E]verything was wet, in less than two hours the water was a foot deep all over our campgrounds."

That same year, another woman wrote with pleasant surprise that the road in the Platte Valley was "as broad as eight or ten common roads in the States, and with very little work [it] could be made one of the most beautiful roads in the world." That road was the Oregon Trail, which was the main route across Nebraska for several decades.

Later Trails

In 1846, members of The Church of Jesus Christ of Latter-day Saints, also called Mormons, left their home in Nauvoo, Illinois, crossed Iowa, and camped on the Missouri River near present-day Omaha. Others joined them, and more than 3,700 people spent the winter there. On their way west, the Mormons followed a trail on the north side of the Platte River, crossing what are now the states of Nebraska and Wyoming to reach their eventual home in Utah. The Mormon Trail was later known as the Mormon/Council Bluffs Road. Fortune hunters heading for California during the gold rush of 1848 and 1849 traveled this route.

Members of The Church of Jesus Christ of Latter-day Saints traveled along the Mormon Trail on their way to Utah.

The U.S. government started the Pony Express in 1860, then described as "the greatest enterprise of modern times." The service lasted only about nineteen months, but, during that time, some four hundred young men and boys on horseback carried mail packets along the route. The entire Pony Express route covered nearly 2,000 miles (3,200 km) between St. Joseph, Missouri, and Sacramento, California.

Settlers left their letters in a prairie mailbox for riders of the Pony Express to pick up and deliver.

Telegraph service was completed across the country in October 1861. This faster and cheaper way to send messages soon put the Pony Express out of business.

The Transcontinental
Railway was com-
pleted in 1869.

Railroads and Highways

Before long, wagon trails and horseback paths gave way to rail-roads. A transcontinental railway had been completed by 1869, and Nebraska was connected to both coasts. The old routes remained but were no longer needed for long-distance travel. By 1880, the new state had nearly half a million residents.

The twentieth century brought automobiles and the roads to drive them on. Motorists could travel from coast to coast on the first transcontinental highway, U.S. Route 30 (the Lincoln Highway). The Oregon Trail had been Nebraska's Main Street. The Lincoln Highway, on the north side of the Platte River, became the most traveled route across Nebraska.

Today's main route through Nebraska is the fast, limited-access Interstate 80. It enters the state at the border of Omaha, extends south to Lincoln, then continues west. From Grand Island to the border of Wyoming, Interstate 80 follows the Oregon and Pony Express Trails through Nebraska. Interstate travelers can cross Nebraska in less than a day; the trek took several weeks by covered wagon.

The thousands of pioneers who crossed Nebraska on their way to western states considered it a great desert. The ones who stayed and put down roots created a state that feeds much of the nation today. Open prairies have become neat, irrigated fields of corn, alfalfa, milo (a grain sorghum), soybeans, and sugar beets. Huge herds of beef cattle roam the western rangelands and are fattened in Nebraska feedlots before going to market. Pigs, sheep, and chickens are also raised in the state.

When you sit down to a big dinner, the chances are good that something on the table came from a Nebraska farm or ranch. Before you begin eating that meal, stop for a minute and think about the adventuresome, courageous, persistent people who made it possible.

Chapter Two

Before It Was Nebraska

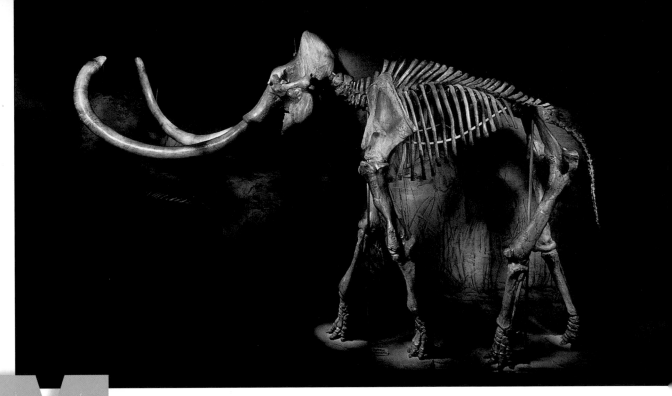

More than half a million years ago, during the Ice Age, great herds of mammoths roamed the Great Plains. As the glaciers that had covered much of North America melted, animals that had lived farther south arrived. Bison (buffalo), camels, and other large animals shared the territory.

Many fossils have been found in Nebraska, Wyoming, and other states and provinces of the Great Plains. Mammoth remains have been found in almost all the counties of Nebraska. Fossils have also been found of other strange, prehistoric mammals that lived there millions of years before them.

The largest known mammoth fossil found anywhere in the world was discovered in Lincoln County, Nebraska. It is on display at the University of Nebraska State Museum in Lincoln. The museum's Elephant Hall has a collection of complete skeletons of all the types of elephants that have lived in North America.

The largest known mammoth fossil is on display in Lincoln.

Opposite. Settlers moving west

Early Communities

There is evidence that people existed in the Great Plains, at least off and on, from about 10,000 years ago. These prehistoric people, called Paleo-Indians, were hunters and gatherers who moved from place to place in search of food. They hunted large herds of bison, which provided a major part of their diet. Arrow points that date from the Stone Age have been found near Scottsbluff, Nebraska. Other archaeological digs in the vicinity have uncovered flint scrapers, bone tools, gouges, and beads that were made by later people.

By about A.D. 400, the group known as the Woodland People had discovered agriculture. They grew corn, vegetables, and sunflowers. They made pottery and used the bones of bison to fashion hoes and other tools.

The Woodland Period continued until about A.D. 900. Until the Europeans arrived in the New World, native peoples continued to migrate to the Great Plains regions, bringing more advanced agricultural practices and settlements.

A Pawnee Indian being attacked by a grizzly bear

The Europeans Arrive

During the early eighteenth century, Spanish explorers and French fur traders came into the region that is now Nebraska. They encountered several different Native American tribes, or nations.

In western Nebraska, there were several tribes within two larger groups: the Dakota and the Cheyenne. They were primarily nomadic.

The Pawnee lived in the central third of Nebraska. They lived in earth lodges gathered together in villages. They grew corn, beans, and squashes in small gardens. Once or twice a year, the whole community traveled to hunt game and lived in tepees made of animal skins.

In the east, between the Pawnee lands and the Missouri River, were several native groups: the Ponca, Omaha, and Oto. Their lifestyles were similar to that of the Pawnee.

None of the European powers recognized that Native Ameri-

Exploration of Nebraska

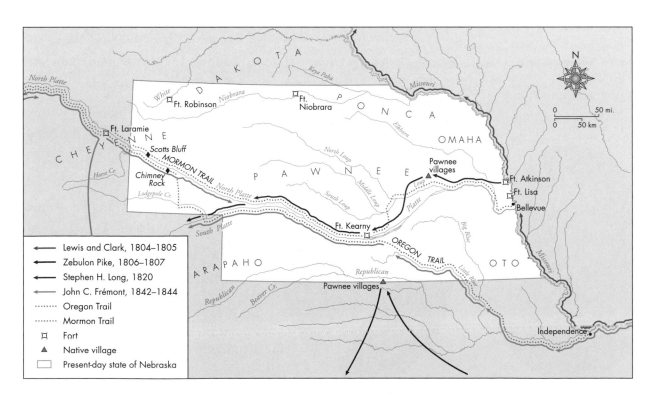

cans had any rights to land in the Americas. Spain, France, and England each wanted to extend its control over North American regions. The British were strongest east of the Mississippi River; France held eastern Canada; Spain was powerful in Mexico and the region that later became the southwestern United States. Wars were fought in Europe and North America over these claims.

In the Treaty of Paris, signed in 1763, all the land west of the Mississippi River claimed by France was ceded to Spain. Most of this land was called the Louisiana Territory. Spain agreed in 1800 to give this territory back to France. In 1803, the United States purchased the Louisiana Territory from the French.

The Louisiana Purchase was the most important event in U.S. history in the early nineteenth century. Remembered as one of President Thomas Jefferson's greatest achievements, the purchase made it possible for the United States to continue its westward expansion.

President Jefferson was anxious to find out just what he had bought. He commissioned Meriwether Lewis and William Clark to lead an expedition from St. Louis up the Missouri River through the Louisiana Territory and across the mountains to the Pacific Ocean. On July 15, 1804, the expedition reached the shore of the Missouri River. Several days later, Lewis and Clark negotiated a treaty with representatives of native Nebraskan tribes before continuing their journey through the region. The explorers named their meeting place

Left: William Clark

Right: Meriwether Lewis

John C. Frémont

American explorer and general John C. Frémont was nicknamed The Great Pathfinder. He did not actually make any new trails to the West, however. He simply followed the routes used by early fur traders. His renown came from the written reports that he and his wife made of their journeys.

From 1842 to 1844, while he was still a lieutenant, Frémont led an exploring expedition through the Platte Valley to the South Pass. The first camp was located 2 miles (3.2 km) south of present-day Plattsmouth.

Native Americans called the Platte River *Nibrathka,* meaning "shallow." Frémont used the English version of the word, Nebraska, to refer to the whole region, and the U.S. Congress adopted the name in organizing the Nebraska Territory. Frémont named several geographic landmarks as he traveled west to California.

In 1856, the settlers of a new town west of Omaha chose to name their community for the Pathfinder. Today, the town of Fremont is the seat of Dodge County. ■

Council Bluff, which is located near present-day Fort Calhoun, Nebraska.

Other early explorers of the Nebraska region were army officers Zebulon Pike, Stephen H. Long, Henry Dodge, and John C. Frémont. Most of them were not impressed by the region. They reported that much of the land was desert and would never make good farmland.

Only a few places along the Missouri River were settled during the first few years of U.S. ownership. In 1812, the American Fur Company set up a trading post on the Missouri River, about 10 miles (16 km) north of Omaha. Bellevue was the site of another trading post founded in 1822. The U.S. Army established Fort Atkinson near present-day Fort Calhoun in 1819.

Fort Kearny was established in 1848 to protect travelers along the Oregon Trail.

More than nine hundred emigrants traveled along the Oregon Trail in 1843. Fort Kearny was established in 1848 to protect the increasing number of travelers, first at Nebraska City and later on the Platte River near the present town of Kearney. By 1850, thousands of pioneers were traveling the Oregon Trail each year on their way to the West. Almost all of the early pioneers' writings mention two of Nebraska's most famous landmarks along the trail: Chimney Rock and Scotts Bluff.

Broken Promises

In 1851, the U.S. government signed a treaty at Fort Laramie (Wyoming) with representatives from half a dozen American Indian tribes in the Great Plains. Boundaries were drawn around sections of land that the government promised would belong to the Plains Indians forever. Most explorers and westward-bound

Pioneers traveling through the Great Plains claimed some of the land that had been promised to Native American tribes.

pioneers considered the region not worth settling, so the negotiators of the treaty thought they were giving the tribes land that had little value.

Eventually, the government broke its promise. Seven states, including Nebraska, were carved out of lands that had been guaranteed to the Plains Indians by the Treaty of Fort Laramie.

Nebraska Territory

Railroad companies were anxious to extend their routes across the United States and wanted Congress to establish a Nebraska Territory. The government granted the companies large tracts of land, which they hoped to sell to settlers looking for farmland. Some of the settlers already there were also in favor of the idea of a

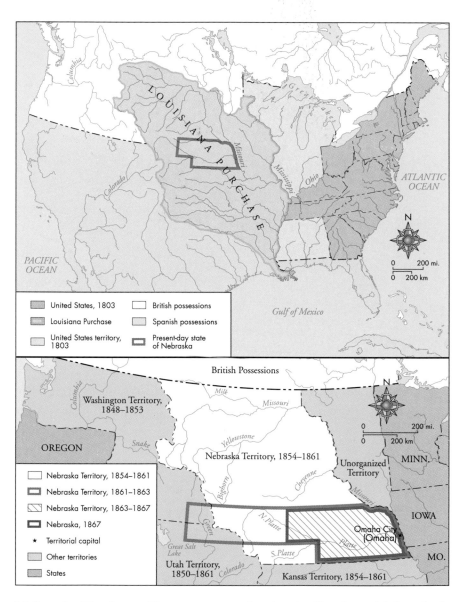

Historical map of Nebraska

Nebraska Territory. They wrote enthusiastically about Nebraska's soil, hoping to attract more farmers to join them.

As Congress was considering creating Nebraska Territory, the controversy over slavery was beginning to heat up in the northern and southern states. The Missouri Compromise of 1820 had admitted two new states: Missouri as a slave state and Maine as a free state. At the same time, it banned slavery in the northern part of the Louisiana Territory, including present-day Nebraska. The intent was to keep a balance between slaveholding and free states.

Pro-slavery advocates were afraid of creating a large territory in which slavery was banned, however. Congress decided to establish two new territories: Kansas and Nebraska. The Kansas-Nebraska Act of 1854 voided part of the Missouri Compromise and gave the new territories the right to decide whether or not slavery would be permitted within their borders. Although slavery was not banned in the Nebraska Territory, there were never many slaves there.

The city of Omaha was also founded in 1854, and the first territorial legislature met in that city in 1855. The number of newcomers in eastern Nebraska increased greatly during the next decade. Nebraska's population grew quickly—from 2,732 in 1854 to 28,841 in 1860.

The Union Pacific depot in Omaha

The Homestead Act

There were two important factors in the settlement of the western United States: the building of railroads through the West and the passage of the Homestead Act in 1862. The Homestead Act granted public land to citizens for a small filing fee, provided that they lived on the claim for five years and cultivated the land. The railroad

Homestead National Monument of America

The Homestead National Monument of America, west of the town of Beatrice, commemorates the settlers who acquired land under the Homestead Act. The 160-acre (65-ha) site includes a cabin, a one-room school named for settler Daniel Freeman, and an exhibit of early farm tools and carriages. Audiovisual programs at the visitor center tell the story of the pioneer settlement, and there are special activities for children as well as a 2.5-mile (4-km) nature trail through a tall-grass prairie and wooded area. ■

companies actively recruited new settlers from the eastern states and from Europe. More than one million people became landowners through this act.

Daniel Freeman of Illinois filed a claim in Nebraska Territory shortly after midnight on January 1, 1863, the day the law went into effect. He acquired a tract of land at Cub Creek in Gage County.

Becoming a State

Nebraska had a mix of territorial governments before it was finally admitted to the United States. Politicians found it difficult to agree on a state constitution. Candidates for state offices fought bitter campaigns. People were asked to vote on various issues, but the election results were very close and raised questions as to the honesty of the count.

Many Nebraskans were anxious to join the United States, and in January 1864, the territorial legislature petitioned Congress to pass legislation to make it possible. The legislature held a special election to approve a state constitution and elect state officers. David Butler was elected governor. On July 4, 1866, Butler called the legislature into session. Two Republicans were chosen as Nebraska's first U.S. senators.

Congress still had not approved Nebraska's statehood. There was strong objection within the U.S. Congress to a provision in the proposed state constitution that restricted voting rights to free white males. In 1866, Congress passed a bill that would admit Nebraska as a state if the objectionable restriction were removed. President Andrew Johnson vetoed the bill, but Congress passed it over his veto. Nebraska was declared the thirty-seventh state on March 1, 1867.

Close Calls

Nebraska was finally admitted as the thirty-seventh state on March 1, 1867—but some important issues had to be resolved first. The people of Nebraska Territory found it difficult to agree on the issues of statehood and slavery, and were evenly divided on the terms of the proposed constitution and who should be governor.

Voting on constitution:
For: 3,938
Against: 3,838

Votes for governor:
Butler (Republican): 4,093
Morton (Democrat): 3,984 ■

CHAPTER THREE

A Pioneer Spirit

A view of the town of Ogallala, which was the end of the Texas cattle drive trail

"Land! Free land!" The cry echoed through the states east of the Mississippi. No longer did almost all the wagon trains carrying families and household possessions travel through Nebraska to destinations farther west. Now many people stayed, lured by the prospect of settling on land of their own. The Homestead Act seemed to open up a bright future of prosperity for farmers. Getting to Nebraska was easier and faster than ever before, too. By 1869, trains could travel on tracks that reached all the way from the East Coast to the West.

Struggles on Farms and Ranches

Nebraska, especially the western part, seemed perfect for herding cattle. The prairie grasses supplied excellent food, and water was abundant. Canyons, ravines, and rocky bluffs provided shelter for the animals in severe weather. Buffalo, elk, and antelope had thrived here for centuries, and cattle could, too.

Opposite: A farmer in his cornfield prays for rain.

Grasshopper Invasions

Nebraska was invaded by grasshoppers several times between 1856 and 1876. They approached in huge clouds, so large and dense that the sun was blacked out. The sound the insects made was as loud as that of a fast freight train.

The creatures destroyed everything in sight. They ate holes in clothing, curtains, and bed linens. Trees, vines, and all other kinds of vegetation were stripped clean. Even a pail of water drawn from a deep well would come up with dozens of insects floating in it.

The infestations were too much for many of the settlers, who finally gave up and moved out. The ragged holes chewed in the cloth covers of their wagons told the story. Some of the discouraged pioneers even scrawled messages on the cloth, such as: "Eaten out by grasshoppers. Going back East to live with wife's folks."

The grasshoppers stopped coming after 1876, just as suddenly and mysteriously as they had appeared. ■

The free-ranging cattle were a menace to farmers, however. The animals knocked down fences and destroyed crops. Feuds between ranchers and farmers sometimes became violent.

Nature was pretty hard on the new Nebraskans, too. Rattlesnakes and prairie fires were constant dangers. In the 1880s, severe blizzards brought great quantities of snow, sleet, and ice. More than half of some herds were destroyed, and their owners were forced into bankruptcy. A decade later, a series of scorching droughts caused great hardship for farmers and herders.

By 1870, there were more than four times as many people in Nebraska as there had been a decade before. Despite all the problems and disappointments faced by many of the settlers, more kept coming. The citizens were eager to go about the business of building a new, progressive state. One of the first priorities was to establish a state university. The University of Nebraska opened in Lincoln in 1871. During the next twenty years, the population multiplied by ten.

The University of Nebraska at Lincoln was established in 1871.

The LaFlesche Sisters

Joseph LaFlesche, chief of the Omaha Reservation from 1853 to 1866, was the father of four remarkable daughters: Susette (left), Rosalie, Marguerite, and Susan. The four women did not always agree, but all were talented representatives of their people and became well known for their achievements. Three of the sisters graduated from Hampton Institute in Virginia, a school established to educate African-Americans and American Indians.

Susette, the oldest, was a writer, orator, and defender of Indian rights. She was a correspondent for the *Omaha World Herald* newspaper and other publications. She traveled extensively and met many distinguished people, including the popular poet Henry Wadsworth Longfellow. Today, a bust of Susette LaFlesche Tibbles is in the Nebraska Hall of Fame.

Rosalie and her husband managed large tracts of Indian lands. They spoke out in favor of self-government for the Omaha people, independent of federal and state agencies.

After graduating from Hampton Institute, Marguerite returned to the reservation as a teacher. She was active in social, political, and educational affairs of Native Americans. One of her projects was to establish library facilities in Walthill, where she and her husband lived.

Susan, the youngest sister, graduated at the head of her class from Woman's Medical College in Philadelphia. She became the first female American Indian doctor of medicine. On the reservation, she served the Omaha people as a physician, interpreter, and teacher. She taught hygienic methods of disease prevention.

Like her sister Susette, Dr. Susan LaFlesche Picotte traveled widely as a public speaker. In 1910, she headed a tribal delegation to Washington, D.C., to lobby for the rights of the Omaha. In 1913, she opened the first American Indian hospital, located in Walthill. The building is now a museum on the National Register of Historic Places. ■

More Broken Promises

For the most part, settlers and the Ponca coexisted peacefully in the area near the mouth of the Niobrara River. In 1858, the Ponca agreed to relinquish most of their lands, holding only a small reserve. They had difficulty living off the land, just as the settlers did.

The federal government made matters worse when it signed a second Treaty of Fort Laramie in 1868. Mistakenly, some of the Ponca lands were promised to the Sioux. The two tribes were already at odds over hunting rights. The nomadic Sioux warriors frequently raided Ponca villages, killing many Ponca.

The government decided to "protect" the Ponca by forcing them to move to Indian Territory (the future state of Oklahoma) with other Nebraska tribes. Living conditions in the territory were terrible. Most of the Indians became sick and many died. It was a sad and shameful period in the history of relationships between the U.S. government and the Native Americans.

Meanwhile, gold had been discovered in Montana. Fortune hunters tramped through Sioux lands in western Nebraska and Wyoming on their way to look for gold. To keep peace, the government moved the Indians to reservations, but many of the young Indians opposed the idea of being confined to these lands. When gold was discovered in the Black Hills (in present-day South Dakota), more conflict arose. The Sioux regarded the Black Hills as sacred. Also, the U.S. government had promised them "absolute and undisturbed use and occupation" of these lands.

Bitter battles were fought between the US Army and the Native Americans. One of the Sioux leaders was a well-respected young man named Crazy Horse. He was one of the leaders at the Battle of the Little Bighorn in 1876. The U.S. Army's Lieutenant Colonel George Custer and most of his men were killed in that famous battle.

The Indians could not hold out indefinitely against the power of the U.S. Army, however, and the Sioux were eventually forced to give up most of their claims. In 1877, Chief Crazy Horse, then thirty-five years old, and several hundred of his followers surrendered at the Red Cloud Agency near Fort Robinson. Crazy Horse was killed by a soldier while he was being led into a jail cell.

The defeat of Chief Crazy Horse, 1877

Buffalo Bill Cody

William Frederick "Buffalo Bill" Cody is one of the most colorful figures in the history of the American West. His name immediately conjures up visions of buffalo hunting, cowboys, rodeos, and the wild frontier.

Cody was born in Scott County, Iowa, in 1846. An expert rider and rifleman, he had countless adventures before he was out of his teens. He started working as a trail hand at age nine and was a messenger boy at Fort Kearny at twelve. He supposedly rode for the Pony Express when he was only fourteen, and legend claims he once rode more than 300 miles (480 km) in twenty-two hours.

During the Civil War, Cody served as an Indian scout for the 7th Kansas calvary. As a buffalo hunter for the railroads (which is how he earned his nickname), Cody claimed to have shot more than four thousand buffalo. In 1872, he guided a buffalo hunting party that included the Grand Duke Alexis, brother of the Russian czar.

Cody had a longtime wish to get into show business. In 1882, he organized a rodeo in North Platte and, the following year, produced his first Wild West show in Omaha. It was wildly successful, and Buffalo Bill's Wild West Show toured the United States and Europe until 1913. Cody built a mansion on his North Platte ranch, Scouts Rest, which is now part of Buffalo Bill State Historical Park.

Cody died in 1917. His memory is alive in many Hollywood movies and television westerns, and his bust is in the Nebraska Hall of Fame. ∎

Fort Robinson

Fort Robinson, on 22,000 acres (8,900 ha), is Nebraska's largest state park. The fort has a colorful—but not always admirable—history. Since its establishment in 1874, it has been a military outpost, cavalry station, frontier Indian agency, training center for Olympic equestrians and K-9 war dogs, and, during World War II, a prisoner of war camp.

Today, the fort is a learning center of Nebraska's nature and history. Historic buildings provide visitors with accommodations, meeting rooms, a restaurant, a visitor center, and museums. There are also hiking and riding trails, a lake, ponds, and other recreational facilities. Evening programs include rodeo games, campfire talks, and presentations of comedy and melodrama at the Post Playhouse. ■

William Jennings Bryan during the 1896 presidential campaign

Two Nebraskan Politicians

Two men kept Nebraska in the headlines in the 1890s and several later decades: William Jennings Bryan (1860–1925) and George William Norris (1861–1944).

Bryan was elected to Congress for two terms, from 1890 to 1894. A so-called silver-tongued orator, he quickly rose to a position of power in the Democratic Party. He was nominated for the presidency by his party three times, but was defeated each time. His fame as an orator continued, and he traveled extensively for thirty-five years giving speeches. He spoke out for the common people, in favor of equal rights, for laws against child labor, and many other causes.

George W. Norris served his state in Washington from 1902 to 1942—for ten years as a member of the House of Representatives and then thirty more as a senator. In 1933, Congress passed Norris's bill to create the Tennessee Valley Authority (TVA), whose goal was to develop the natural resources of the Tennessee River Valley. In 1934, Norris helped pass an amendment to the Nebraska Constitution that created a one-house state legislature.

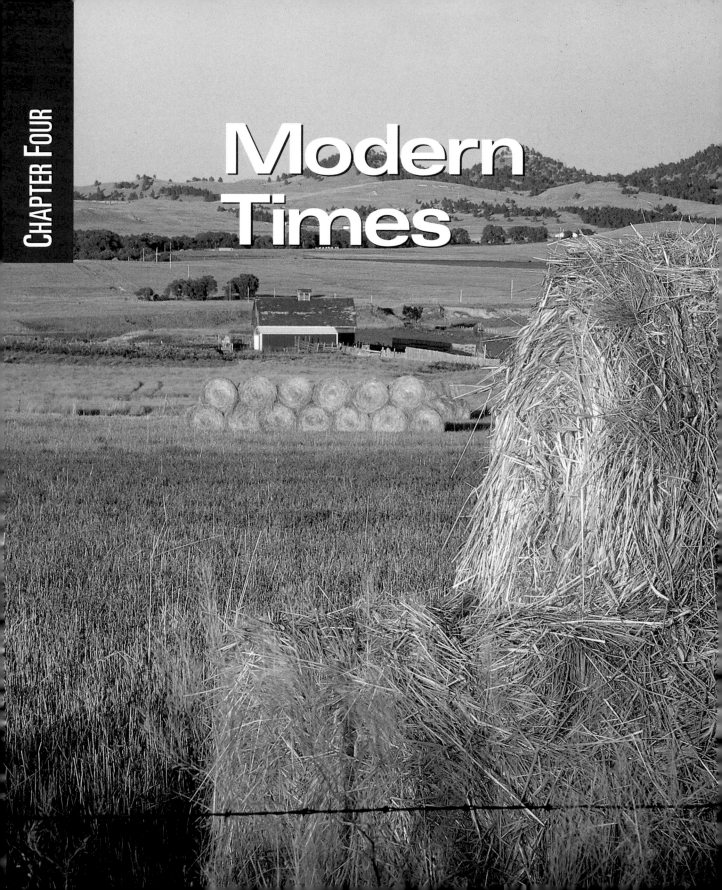

CHAPTER FOUR

Modern Times

Another 300,000 people moved into Nebraska between 1900 and 1930. The cattle industry developed rapidly, and farm production increased through the use of modern agricultural methods.

In 1914, as World War I started in Europe, vigorous debates were heard in Nebraska about whether the United States should become involved in the war. The many German-born people and their descendants living in Nebraska felt a loyalty to their homeland. Some Nebraskans simply supported peace over war, and others didn't understand why America had to get involved. But when the U.S. government declared war in 1917, more than 57,000 young Nebraska men and women joined the armed forces.

Back home, motivated both by patriotism and high prices, Nebraska's farmers went into high gear.

The years after the war were bad times for agriculture in Nebraska, however. Wartime demand had encouraged farmers to put more land into cultivation. After the war, however, the demand diminished and prices plummeted. At the same time, operating

President Woodrow Wilson urges Congress to declare war in 1917.

Opposite: Bales of hay at sunset, near Chadron

Father Flanagan and Boys Town

Edward Joseph Flanagan (above, center) was born in Ireland in 1886. He came to the United States at the age of eighteen, went to college, and then studied in New York, Italy, and Austria to become a Roman Catholic priest. While assigned to parishes in the towns of O'Neill and Omaha, Nebraska, he soon realized how he could make a difference in people's lives.

Father Flanagan believed his best work was helping homeless boys who had no one to care for them. In 1917, he rented a house in Omaha to take care of five boys. He raised enough money to buy the 160-acre 45(65-ha) Overlook Farm 10 miles (16 km) out of town. He moved his Boys Town to its present location in 1921.

Thousands of young people have been saved from the streets since Father Flanagan first started to make his dream come true. The whole world became aware of Boys Town and its benefits to needy youngsters when the movie *Boys Town* was made in 1938. Spencer Tracy played Father Flanagan and won an Oscar for the performance. Mickey Rooney starred as one of the boys.

Father Flanagan died in 1948, but his work goes on. Boys Town is still a haven for boys, and now for girls also. Five to seven foster brothers and sisters live together in family homes, and each home is headed by a married couple. There are schools, a vocational training center, athletic facilities, and a music hall on campus. Visitors can see Boys Town's famous statue: one boy carrying another and the inscription: "He ain't heavy, Father, he's m' brother." Father Flanagan's home is also on view, furnished as it was when he lived there from 1927 through 1941.

The Boys Town National Research Hospital opened in downtown Omaha in 1975. Boys Town "mini-campuses" have been established in several other states, with plans to have seventeen Boys Town USA sites in operation by the year 2000. ■

costs rose dramatically. When the Great Depression swept over the nation in the 1930s, the state's economy was near collapse. Some help came from various agencies of the federal government, established under President Franklin D. Roosevelt's New Deal.

During World War II (1939–1945), Nebraska was again called on to produce great quantities of food to feed the nation. For a while, the state once again enjoyed prosperity. Farms and ranches in Nebraska greatly increased their production. Manufacturers produced war supplies worth more than $1.2 billion.

Agriculture after World War II

The prosperity created by World War II continued, for the most part, through the last half of the twentieth century. Agriculture has

Nebraska's fertile fields helped feed the nation during World War II.

continued to be a major source of income for Nebraska, although fewer people are now employed on farms. Because of larger and more efficient farm machinery, increased irrigation, and better agricultural methods, less human power is required to produce as much, or more, farm product. As farm jobs became more scarce, many people moved from rural areas to the cities. Today, there are fewer farms than there used to be, but the average size is much greater.

The Pick-Sloan Missouri Basin Project, passed by Congress in 1944, authorized the creation of flood-control dams, reservoirs, and hydroelectric plants in Nebraska and other Missouri River states. Since then, there has been a spectacular growth in irrigation across the state. New irrigation technology and methods of drawing water

Gerald Rudolph Ford

Gerald R. Ford was born in Omaha on July 14, 1913. He became the first Nebraska-born U.S. president on August 9, 1974.

Ford was originally named Leslie Lynch King Jr. After his parents divorced, he and his mother moved to Grand Rapids, Michigan. Ford's mother remarried, and his name changed when he was adopted by his stepfather.

Ford was a Republican member of the U.S. Congress for twenty-five years. In 1973, Richard M. Nixon appointed him vice president to replace Spiro T. Agnew, who had resigned. Ford became president when Nixon resigned in 1974. He ran for reelection in 1976 but lost to Jimmy Carter of Georgia.

During his retirement, the former president has been ready and willing to help his successors in many ways. A commemorative rose garden has been created at the site of President Ford's birthplace in Omaha. ■

from underground aquifers have made thousands of acres of dry land productive. Environmentalists, however, are concerned about using so much water for irrigation and about pollution of the water supply from farm runoff.

Education in the Sixties

Educational opportunities for Nebraskans expanded in the 1960s and early 1970s. State-supported educational television began in 1963, and Nebraska became one of the first states to broadcast educational programming to the entire state. In 1968, the University of Nebraska in Lincoln was reorganized to include additional campuses in Omaha and Curtis (and later at Kearney). A community-college system was established in 1971.

Recession in the Eighties
and into the Nineties

The entire nation suffered a financial recession in the 1980s. In Nebraska, land values dropped sharply, and some farmers had to sell out. In 1987, the state legislature authorized tax incentives to lure new businesses and new jobs to the state.

Agricultural technology has continued to develop into the 1990s. Farming has become increasingly mechanized with huge, computerized farming equipment guided by satellite geopositioning aiding farmworkers. As a result, fewer people are needed to farm larger acreages. Many unemployed workers have moved to the cities in search of work. Even with this reduction in farmworkers, Nebraska remains primarily an agricultural state.

Nebraska's Firsts

■ The 911 system of emergency communications, now used nationwide, was developed and first used in Lincoln.

■ The research and development of air ambulance services (below) began in Nebraska.

■ Automatic teller machines (ATMs) at grocery-store counters were first used in Lincoln.

■ Fort Atkinson was the first military post and had the first school west of the Missouri River (in 1820).

■ Nebraska was the first state to complete its segment of the nation's interstate highway system—a 445-mile (716-km) portion of Interstate 80.

■ Whittier Junior High in Lincoln was the first junior high school in the nation.

■ Nebraska was the first state to use an automated visible voting board to record legislative votes.

■ The University of Nebraska was the first land-grant college west of the Missouri River to offer graduate-level course work.

■ Buffalo Bill Cody held the nation's first rodeo at his Scouts Rest Ranch in North Platte to celebrate the Fourth of July in 1882

■ The 1986 race for governor, in which Republican Kay Orr (below) defeated Democrat Helen Boosalis, was the first gubernatorial race in U.S. history in which both major candidates were women. Orr's election made her the first Republican woman governor in U.S. history.

■ Among the products invented or developed in Nebraska are Kool-Aid, Vise-Grip pliers, the Cushman motor scooter, and the Reuben sandwich. ■

Entering the Twenty-first Century

Television, satellite dishes, superhighways, videos, computers, and the Internet have all brought great changes to rural Nebraska during the last few decades. Some ranch or farm families may live quite a distance from their closest neighbors, just as their pioneer ancestors did, but they are still in touch and informed. With the flip of a switch or the turn of a dial, Nebraskans stay close to the rest of the world.

Many farm families enjoy the convenience of satellite television.

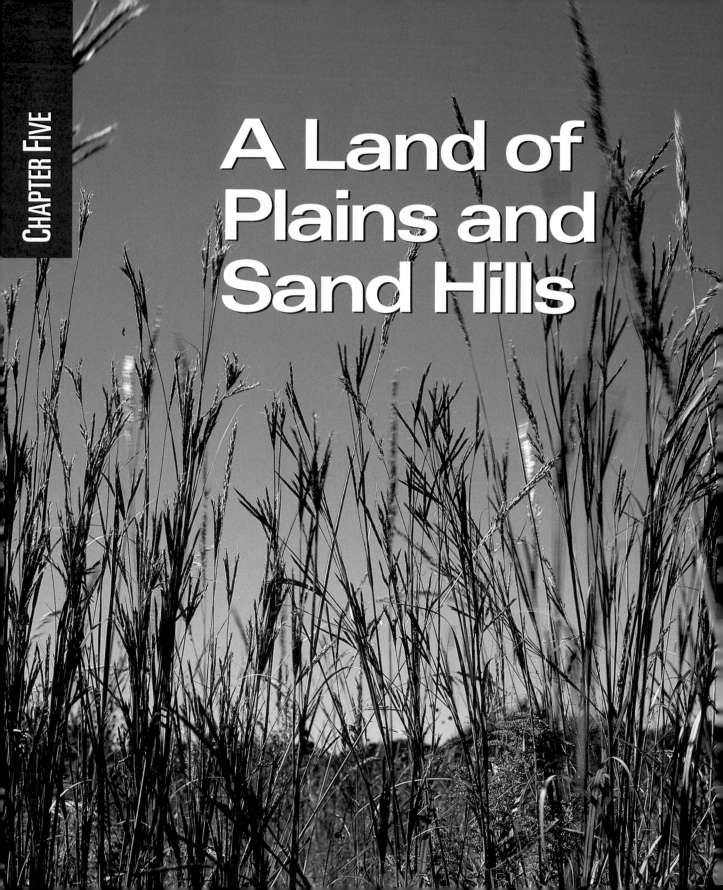

CHAPTER FIVE

A Land of Plains and Sand Hills

Soybean fields in early morning, near Falls City

The land and the climate of Nebraska were not very kind to the early pioneers. Droughts, hailstorms, and hoards of grass-hoppers destroyed crops in summer; blizzards made life almost unbearable in winter. But many of the hardy settlers held onto their dream that times would be better. Someday, they believed, it would be possible to make a living from this land, harsh though it seemed.

They were right. Those who stuck it out transformed a land once called the Great American Desert into a leading farming and ranching state. In Nebraska, a larger percentage of total land is used for producing crops and livestock than in any other state.

Land Forms

Nebraska's land slopes gently upward from east to west. Near Rulo in Richardson County, along the Missouri River, it is about 840 feet (255 m) above sea level. The highest elevation, in the southwestern Panhandle in Kimball County, is more than 1 mile (1.6 kilometers) high.

Opposite: Prairie grasses blowing in the wind

Eastern Nebraska is part of the Central Lowlands that extend into the neighboring states of South Dakota, Iowa, Missouri, and Kansas. This region covers about one-fifth of the state. There are deep deposits of loess, a rich, windblown soil that is excellent for agriculture. The rolling land, once covered by glaciers, is cut by many rivers and streams. All these waterways flow into the Missouri River, which forms the eastern and northeastern border of Nebraska.

The western 80 percent of the state is within the Great Plains. The Great Plains stretch from northern Canada to southern Texas and include parts of ten states in the central United States. The

Nebraska's Geographical Features

Total area; rank	77,359 sq. mi. (200,359 sq km); 16th
Land; rank	76,878 sq. mi. (199,114 sq km); 15th
Water; rank	481 sq. mi. (1,246 sq km); 39th
Inland water; rank	481 sq. mi. (1,246 sq km); 33rd
Geographic center	Custer, 10 miles (16 km) northwest of Broken Bow
Highest point	Panorama Point, Johnson Township, 5,424 feet (1,653 m)
Lowest point	480 feet (146 m), at the Missouri River
Largest city	Omaha
Longest river	Missouri River, 450 miles (724 km)
Population; rank	1,584,687 (1990 census); 36th
Record high temperature	118°F (48°C) at Minden on July 24, 1936; at Hartington on July 17, 1936; 1936; and at Geneva on July 15, 1934
Record low temperature	−47°F (−44°C) at Camp Clarke, near Northport, on February 12, 1899
Average July temperature	76°F (24°C)
Average January temperature	23°F (−5°C)
Average annual precipitation	12 inches (30.5 cm)

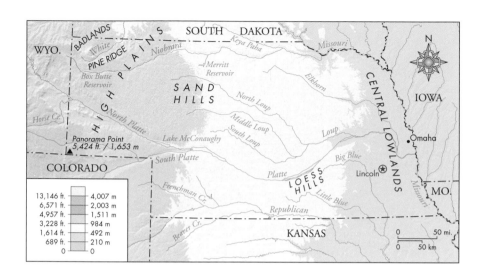

Nebraska's topography

Great Plains region of Nebraska contains three subdivisions: the Loess Hills, the Sand Hills, and the High Plains.

Loess covers the soil in the eastern part of the Great Plains. North of the Platte River, the plains have eroded into hills and ridges separated by valleys.

The Sand Hills are north of the Platte River in central Nebraska. They cover about one-fourth of the state. Winds formed low hills and ridges of fine sand, most of them covered with grasses. The Sand Hills region of Nebraska is the largest area of sand dunes in North America and one of the largest in the world. Only the Sahara and Arabian Deserts are larger expanses of sand. Streams and wells supply abundant water. Cattle ranching is the main business in this region, as the grasses make excellent feed.

Conservation of the grass cover is an important concern in the Sand Hills. Overgrazing and extensive irrigated farming could destroy the precious vegetation.

The western part of Nebraska is known as the Panhandle. Most

The moon setting over the Sand Hills

of the land is a part of the High Plains, which extend into Wyoming and Colorado. Hills in the Nebraskan High Plains rise to an elevation of more than 1 mile (1.6 km) above sea level. The Wildcat Hills and the Pine Ridge are covered with evergreen trees.

The unusual landscape in the far northwestern area of the state is part of the rugged Badlands, which comprises a large region of South Dakota. Erosion has scoured steep, rocky hills almost bare and carved them into strange shapes.

Rivers and Lakes

Two major rivers—the Missouri and the Platte—have shaped Nebraska's history. The Missouri is the second-longest river in the United States. It flows from southern Montana in a southeastern direction to join the Mississippi (the longest river in the United

Chimney Rock and Scotts Bluff

During the mid-nineteenth century, thousands of pioneers traveled west by wagon train along the Oregon Trail. In letters they sent to friends and relatives back home, they described several natural land formations they had seen along the way, advising others setting out to keep a lookout on the horizon for them. The early trailblazers gave these remarkable landmarks names: Courthouse Rock, Jail Rock, Chimney Rock, Scotts Bluff, Dome Rock. Lumbering along in wagon trains, the pioneers had them in their view for days. Today, tourists can whiz past all of them on U.S. Highway 26 in just a few hours.

Chimney Rock (above), a steeplelike spire about 500 feet (152 m) high, is a national historic site. An early pioneer observed that the name was chosen well: "One might almost expect to see smoke or steam jetting from the summit," he wrote. The rock can be reached only on foot, and the trail is difficult to travel. The visitor center near the highway has an interpretive exhibit, with a miniature display of what it was like to make the trek by wagon train.

Scotts Bluff (below), a national monument, is 23 miles (37 km) west of Chimney Rock. It was a popular campsite along the trail. The Sioux name for it meant "the hill that is hard to go around." The rock was named for Hiram Scott, a fur trader who was abandoned by other members of his expedition and died near the foot of the bluff.

Tourists can hike or drive to the top of the bluff for a spectacular view of the surrounding plains. Ruts made by thousands of wagon wheels during the great westward migration of the nineteenth century are still visible. Displays and exhibits in the Oregon Trail Museum provide information about the history of the trail, the early fur traders, and the Pony Express. There are also paintings and photographs by the artist William Henry Jackson. Jackson drew sketches of the bluff from his campsite in 1866. The artist returned to the trail many times in later years, lugging a heavy camera to take photographs along the trail. ■

States) north of St. Louis. The Missouri forms the eastern border and part of the northeastern border of Nebraska. The Missouri was a major means of transportation into the west for early explorers and pioneers.

The Platte River and its two branches—the North Platte and South Platte Rivers—together cross the entire state. The branches meet at the town of North Platte.

The Platte River crosses the entire state of Nebraska.

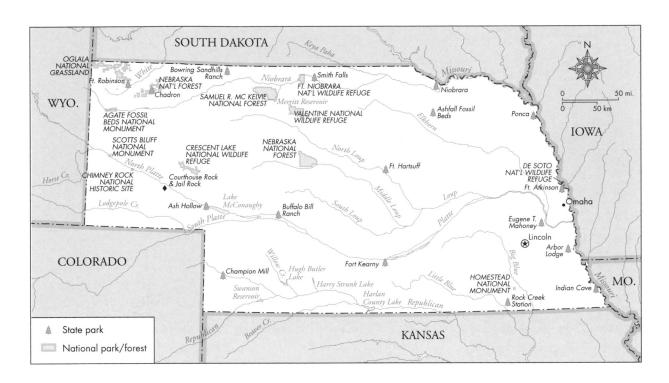

The map shows Nebraska's parks and forests. Labels include:

SOUTH DAKOTA

Keya Paha

OGLALA NATIONAL GRASSLAND

White

Bowring Sandhills Ranch

NEBRASKA NAT'L FOREST

Ft. Robinson

Chadron

Niobrara

Smith Falls

FT. NIOBRARA NAT'L WILDLIFE REFUGE

Missouri

Niobrara

SAMUEL R. MC KELVIE NATIONAL FOREST

Merritt Reservoir

WYO.

AGATE FOSSIL BEDS NATIONAL MONUMENT

VALENTINE NATIONAL WILDLIFE REFUGE

Ashfall Fossil Beds

Elkhorn

Ponca

IOWA

SCOTTS BLUFF NATIONAL MONUMENT

CRESCENT LAKE NATIONAL WILDLIFE REFUGE

NEBRASKA NATIONAL FOREST

North Loup

North Platte

Horse Cr.

CHIMNEY ROCK NATIONAL HISTORIC SITE

Courthouse Rock & Jail Rock

Ft. Hartsuff

Middle Loup

Loup

DE SOTO NAT'L WILDLIFE REFUGE

Ft. Atkinson

Lodgepole Cr.

Ash Hollow

Lake McConaughy

Buffalo Bill Ranch

South Loup

Platte

Omaha

Eugene T. Mahoney

Big Blue

South Platte

Lincoln

Arbor Lodge

COLORADO

Willow Cr.

Hugh Butler Lake

Fort Kearny

Champion Mill

Harry Strunk Lake

Little Blue

HOMESTEAD NATIONAL MONUMENT

Indian Cave

MO.

Swanson Reservoir

Harlan County Lake

Republican

Rock Creek Station

Missouri

Republican

Beaver Cr.

KANSAS

0   50 mi.
0   50 km

State park

National park/forest

The Platte River is not deep enough for navigation, but westward-bound settlers created trails that followed its shores. Today the river is a major source of water for irrigation, recreation, and hydroelectric power. Other important rivers are the Niobrara in the northern part of the state, the Republican in the south, and the Big Blue in the southeast.

Nebraska has more usable water than any other state. There are 22,000 miles (35,406 km) of flowing streams. Hundreds of small and shallow lakes can be found in the Sand Hills. Large lakes in Nebraska have been created by building dams in the rivers. Lake McConaughy, the largest, is in the North Platte River just north of Ogallala.

Nebraska's parks and forests

Lake McConaughy, in the North Platte River, is the largest lake in Nebraska.

The soil of the Sand Hills absorbs and holds rainfall, which creates vast underground reservoirs of ground water. The Ogallala Aquifer is a valuable source of water for irrigation. It is estimated to contain enough of a supply to cover the entire state with 34 feet (10 m) of water.

Environmental Concerns

Wise use of Nebraska's natural resources—especially soil and water—is critically important to the state's economy and welfare. The major danger to the environment is the contamination of groundwater from fertilizers, pesticides, and animal wastes. Migratory birds are threatened by the draining of wetlands and by dams and irrigation projects.

The state government has created natural-resource districts to oversee local conservation efforts. Laws have been passed to regulate how chemicals are applied to the soil.

Climate

Nebraska's climate is not what one would call mild. Temperatures range from severe cold in the winter to blistering heat in summer. Abrupt and violent changes in weather occur in the forms of thunderstorms, tornadoes, blizzards, and hailstorms. Temperatures and rainfall vary quite a lot from year to year.

A storm brewing over Petersburg

The greatest natural hazards for humans and animals in Nebraska are the occasional blizzards, which sometimes appear after spring has begun. On the other hand, tornadoes are more destructive to property. Nebraska has an average of more than thirty tornadoes a year.

Pleasant days in spring and fall, low humidity, long growing seasons, and excellent agricultural land are assets that make living in Nebraska worth the endurance of extremes.

Trees, Grasses, and Wildflowers

Most of Nebraska is not wooded, but there is a lush growth of deciduous (leaf-bearing) trees all along the Missouri River. The eastern half of the state has scattered spots of woodlands near rivers and streams.

Ponderosa pines in the Soldier Creek Wilderness Area

The Man Who Founded Arbor Day

In the days of the pioneers, Nebraska was nearly treeless; the prairie and the sand hills seemed to stretch out forever. Although people are concerned that forests are being cut down faster than they are being replanted, Nebraska has many more trees today than it had in the 1860s.

Much of the credit goes to J. Sterling Morton, a newspaper editor who came to the Nebraska Territory with his wife in 1854. The couple spent their first winter in a log cabin, then moved to Nebraska City. They acquired a 160-acre (65-ha) parcel of land and built a simple frame house. The Mortons beautified their new property by planting ornamental trees and shrubs as well as an apple orchard.

Morton was outspoken about politics, economics, and social issues. He was active in territorial and state politics, but his most lasting influence resulted from his love of trees and agriculture. While serving as president of the Nebraska state board of agriculture, Mortonproposed the idea of setting aside a special day each year for planting trees. On April 10,

1872, the governor proclaimed the first Arbor Day. The legislature made it an official holiday and changed the date to Morton's birthday, April 22. Most states and Canadian provinces have since adopted the custom, although not all of them observe the holiday on the same day. Schoolchildren, especially, enjoy planting trees to celebrate Arbor Day.

In 1893, President Grover Cleveland appointed Morton his secretary of agriculture. After retiring from this post, Morton continued to speak and write about current issues until his death, in 1902.

Morton's house, Arbor Lodge, was greatly enlarged over the years. One of his sons, Joy Morton, founder of Morton Salt Company, deeded the fifty-two-room mansion to the state in 1923. Arbor Lodge State Park attracts many visitors, especially on Arbor Day. A bust of Morton is on display in the Nebraska Hall of Fame. ■

Oak, elm, ash, cottonwood, and willow trees are most common. A pine forest extends across the northwestern corner of Nebraska. Ponderosa pines, red cedars, and more than twenty-five other species of trees, forty-four types of shrubs, and five kinds of vines grow in this region. The Pine Ridge section of the Nebraska National Forest in the northwestern part of the state is a natural forest. There are also two national forests in the Sand Hills created by the planting of thousands of acres of pines.

Prairie grasses grow on much of the land that is not farmed. From a distance, a prairie may look like a sea of similar types of wild grasses. Looking closer, however, you'll find grasses of many different colors, sizes, and heights. In general, tall grasses grow in the eastern part of the state, shorter varieties grow in the west.

Dutchman's-breeches

Grasslands used for grazing cattle must be carefully tended, reseeded when necessary, fertilized, and protected from weeds, pests, and erosion caused by overgrazing.

Throughout Nebraska, flowering shrubs and delicate woodland wildflowers burst into bloom to usher in the spring. Color begins to appear in late March, even though wintry winds and cold rains are still hanging around. The tiny white-and-pink Virginia spring beauty (a native of Nebraska, despite its name) is the first to appear. Bloodroot, Dutchman's-breeches, and violets—white and blue varieties—follow. Wild plum trees, covered with white blossoms in spring, grow in most parts of the state.

In May, the grasslands begin to turn green. Yellow violets, blue phlox, columbine, and many other wildflowers add color to the prairies. The High Plains are brightened by the lavender-colored pasque flower, a bluish beauty that grows atop a fuzzy stem.

A pronghorn antelope

Wildlife

Before the Europeans arrived in the early eighteenth century, American Indians shared the woods and prairies of Nebraska with great herds of bison and many types of smaller animals, such as deer, antelope, coyote, and beaver. Grouse and quail were plentiful, too. Today buffalo are only found on game preserves or wherever farmers and ranchers are raising them. There are three Indian reservations and fifteen wildlife refuges and preserves in the state.

Sandhill Cranes

They arrive every year, thousands and thousands of them, on their annual visit to the Platte River valley. They are on a journey to the far northern parts of Canada, Alaska, and Siberia, but they pause for a few weeks in late February, March, and early April at their favorite stopover. As they approach, they fill the sky in huge V-formations, like strange gliding aircraft. Then they seem to parachute to the ground, legs dangling. The sandhill cranes have come back again.

Cranes follow certain routines in their lives. They generally have one mate for life, and the couples are very protective of each other. They live in communities that travel the same migration paths and return to the same winter and summer homes each year. Some sandhill cranes live permanently in Florida, Georgia, Mississippi, and Cuba. Most of the birds that nest in northern regions, however, are migratory. These birds make their winter homes in Mexico and the southwestern United States. More than three-quarters of the total migrating population come through Nebraska each year. Groups arrive on the sandbars of the Platte at different times, stay a few weeks, and depart, again in groups.

Nebraska offers great banquets to the long-legged, long-necked birds. During their stay, they stuff themselves on small birds, eggs, mice, crayfish, lizards, insects, berries, seeds, and grain. Crowds of them spend their leisure time idly soaring overhead. On land, they often amuse themselves by dancing about. On their journey south in autumn, large flocks are seen in the western part of the state, where there is plenty of corn to eat.

Different species and sub-species of cranes live in many places in the world. In some Asian countries, cranes are regarded as symbols of a long life and happy marriage, so it is considered good luck if a pair of cranes builds its nest near one's home. ■

About ten thousand pronghorn antelope live in northern and northeastern Nebraska. White-tailed deer, bobcats, foxes, badgers, raccoons, and other small animals are also common. Tiny prairie dogs burrow beneath the soil and create homes with several "rooms." These social animals live in communities.

The Sand Hills have one of the last and largest expanses of native prairie in the Great Plains, and the state's woodlands and wetlands are excellent habitats for feeding and breeding. Because of these factors and because Nebraska is in the center of the nation, birds travel into and across the state from all directions. Canada geese, mallard ducks, and other migratory birds stop to rest in Nebraska on their way to and from their winter homes.

Not all the birds in Nebraska are just passing through, however. More than one thousand bald eagles make their winter home in the valleys of the Platte, Missouri, and Niobrara Rivers. Many species of raptors, water birds, and songbirds also live in the state year-round.

Prairie dogs

A Canada goose

CHAPTER SIX

Here and There in Nebraska

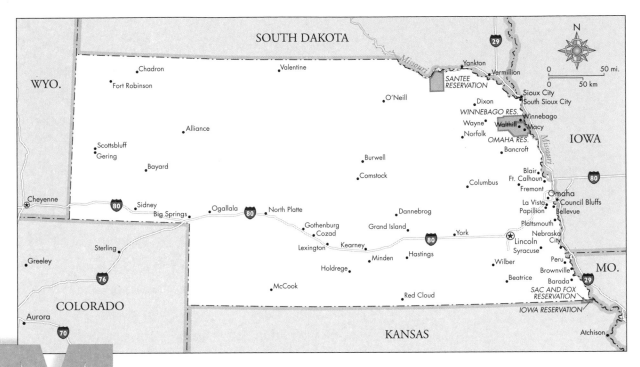

Nebraska's cities and
interstate

M ost of Nebraska has a great deal of open space and
very few people. About one-third of the state's
population is concentrated in the two largest cities, Omaha and
Lincoln. All of the other cities and towns have fewer than 50,000
residents.

The towns in the southeast, near the Missouri River, were settled first. Wagon trails heading west followed the Platte River, and
new settlements grew up along the way. Later towns developed
along the railroads. In general, as one travels west in Nebraska, the
towns are fewer, smaller, and farther apart. Some of the big ranches
are as far as 50 miles (80 km) from the nearest town.

Omaha and Its Surroundings

Omaha, Nebraska's largest city, is a leading business, cultural,
educational, and medical center for the region. Settled in 1854, its

Opposite: The Omaha
skyline

location on the Missouri River made it a natural entry point and supply center for the westward migration. For many years, Omaha's busy livestock market and meat-processing plants formed a major part of its commercial business. More recently, the city has become a thriving, diversified business center with a very low unemployment rate. Today some of its major businesses are telecommunications, transportation, insurance, and food processing.

Omaha was named for the Native American people who lived there until they gave up their lands to settlers. Fort Atkinson, north of the city, was built in 1820 to protect the interests of the newcomers and to promote good relations with the natives. The fort burned in 1827 but was reconstructed and is now a state historical park.

Tourists have many attractions to choose among when visiting Omaha. Two of the favorites are the Henry Doorly Zoo, the most popular attraction in the state, and the Joslyn Art Museum.

A few points of interest in Omaha have the word *Ak-Sar-Ben* as a part of their name. It stands for *Nebraska,* spelled backward.

Lincoln

Omaha was the capital of the Territory of Nebraska. When the people decided on statehood, however, a debate began as to where the capital should be. Although Omaha was still the logical choice— it had more residents than any other area and the best transportation facilities—some state legislators were determined to find a new site for the state capital.

The new site was to be named for President Abraham Lincoln. Only thirty people lived there at the time, but as government

Opposite: The Lied Jungle is located in the Henry Doorly Zoo, one of Nebraska's most popular places.

The Tower of the Plains in Lincoln

offices moved from Omaha to the new town of Lincoln, the population rocketed to five hundred.

Lincoln is the second-largest city in Nebraska. The state government is housed in a tall building nicknamed the Tower of the Plains. Completed in 1932, Nebraska's capitol is regarded as one of the most beautiful public buildings in the nation.

When the University of Nebraska opened its doors in Lincoln in 1871, it had only twenty students. Today, the university has more than 24,000 students, as well as research facilities and

The University of Nebraska

extension services throughout the state. The main campus is in Lincoln, with others in Omaha, Kearney, and Curtis.

Much of the business in Lincoln is centered on the state government and the university, but the city is also a grain market and a manufacturing, insurance, and financial center.

Pioneers Park Nature Center gives visitors a peek at what Nebraska looked like before all the people moved in. There are unspoiled woodlands, wetlands, and prairie. A herd of bison as well as elk, white-tailed deer, red foxes, wild turkeys, and owls can be seen from the trails.

The Southeast Corner

Gently rolling hills make up the landscape of southeastern Nebraska. One town south of Omaha has the interesting name of

The Baradas

The town of Barada, near the southeast corner of Nebraska, was named for a real person. Michael Barada, a European who claimed the title of count, lived on the Omaha reservation with his wife, Laughing Water. Some sources say he was from Paris, others that he was Spanish.

Their son, Antoine (right), had the reputation of being "the strongest man who ever roamed the shores of the Missouri River." Many stories of his strength have been told, most of them no doubt greatly exaggerated. Once he supposedly pulled loose a large boat stranded on a sandbar. Another time he picked up a 400-pound (181-kg) boulder.

Just as there is confusion about where Michael Barada came from, it is not known whether the town of Barada was named for the father or the son. But it doesn't really matter. Both of them were colorful characters in Nebraska's early history. ■

Weeping Water. The town was known to early French trappers as *L'Eau Qui Pleure,* which is the same name in French. A stream flows through the town that at one time made a mournful sound as it flowed over a rocky bed. Several legends have been told about how the town got its name. One was about a battle between two rival Native American groups in which all the warriors were killed. Each year on the anniversary of the battle, women and children from both groups met at the battle site and cried so many tears that a stream was formed.

Two of Nebraska's best-known citizens lived in this part of the state. Bess Streeter Aldrich, who wrote many popular novels about the lives of the pioneers, lived in Elmwood. Nebraska City was the home of J. Sterling Morton, founder of Arbor Day.

Rock Creek Station State Historical Park is south of Lincoln, near the Kansas border. Large ruts made by wagon trains more than

Opposite: The stream that flows through Weeping Water

Cozad

Halfway across Nebraska is the small farming town of Cozad. It was named for John Jackson Cozad, a land speculator from Ohio who worked hard for many years to build the town and attract settlers to it. The well-known Nebraska writer Mari Sandoz told about the many ups and downs of his life in her book *Son of a Gamblin' Man.* Late in Cozad's life he was involved in a shooting battle and had to leave the territory in disgrace.

Cozad's youngest son, Robert Henry, was an artist. He dropped his last name and became famous as Robert Henri. He founded a group of eight artists called The Eight, or the Ashcan School, known for their realistic paintings of cities. ■

one hundred years ago can be seen here. The visitor center has exhibits about the Oregon Trail and the Pony Express. Visitors take rides in an ox-drawn wagon.

A river vessel that helped dredge the channel in the Missouri River is now the Captain Meriwether Lewis Museum of River History, in Brownville. On display are steam engines, boilers, sleeping quarters for fifty-two men, and a pilot house. Brownville was the location of the U.S. Land Office. This is where Daniel Freeman filed his homestead claim, considered to be the first such claim filed in the United States.

Northeastern Nebraska

Often called Lewis and Clark Country, northeastern Nebraska lies between the Platte River on the south and the Missouri on the east and north. The Lewis and Clark expedition traveled up the Missouri along the edge of this section of the state. It has rolling hills in the eastern and grassy plains in the western part of the region.

The DeSoto National Wildlife Refuge lies on both sides of the Missouri, in Iowa and Nebraska. This is a wonderful place for viewing migratory ducks and geese, as well as occasional bald eagles.

The Omaha and Winnebago Indian Reservations are in Thurston County. Bancroft, on the edge of the Omaha Reservation, was the home of Nebraska's poet laureate, John G. Neihardt. Dr. Susan LaFlesche Picotte opened the first Indian hospital in Walthill, a small town in the reservation. The Winnebago people hold a pow-wow each July, and Macy is the host town for the Omaha Powwow each August.

Migrating snow geese at the DeSoto National Wildlife Refuge

Near Dixon is Tarbox Hollow Living Prairie, where a herd of a hundred buffalo graze on the tall grass. Summer visitors can ride close to the animals in a covered wagon.

South of Niobrara is an amazing archaeological site, in Ashfall Fossil Beds State Historical Park. About ten million years ago a volcano erupted in what is now Idaho. The lava ash that fell on this region of Nebraska killed and buried countless prehistoric birds and animals. The story of the fossils found here is told and interpreted in a visitors center. This is one of the most important paleontological finds on the continent.

One of the volunteers at the Stuhr Museum in Grand Island

South-central Nebraska

An 80-mile (129-km) stretch along the Platte River draws thousands of nature-loving tourists each spring. They come to see the millions of ducks and geese and more than half a million sandhill cranes that stop here every spring during their northbound migration. There are several viewing areas near Grand Island and Kearney.

Grand Island, on Interstate 80 and the Platte River, is Nebraska's fourth largest city. The Stuhr Museum of the Prairie Pioneer is a living history museum of early life in Nebraska. There are two exhibit buildings and more than seventy original structures brought in from surrounding areas. One of the homes is the small cottage where the movie star Henry Fonda was born. His voice can be heard narrating an orientation film about the museum.

South of Grand Island is Hastings, the scene of a notorious murder trial in 1879. A vicious feud in Custer County, between homesteaders and cattlemen, led by a rancher named Print Olive, resulted in murders that shocked the whole nation. The shock may have helped bring about changes, however. Tensions between ranchers and farmers seemed to calm down after the incident.

Farther south is Red Cloud, home of Nebraska's most famous author, Willa Cather. Several of her novels were set in this town. Her home is a state historic site.

Willa Cather's home in Red Cloud

West of Grand Island is Kearney. Fort Kearny, named for a U.S. Army brigadier general, was the first army post on the Oregon Trail. The town was named for the fort, but for some unknown reason the spelling was changed. There are two excellent museums in Kearney: the Trails and Rails Museum and the Museum of Nebraska Art.

The Trails and Rails Museum in Kearney

Minden, south of Kearney, is known for the Harold Warp Pioneer Village. Designed to tell the story of America since 1830, there are twenty-eight buildings on 20 acres (8 ha). Included are a sod house, one-room schoolhouse, railroad depot, blacksmith shop, and other structures once common but fast disappearing from the American landscape.

The north and south branches of the Platte River meet in North Platte. William "Buffalo Bill" Cody lived here. His home, Scouts Rest Ranch, is in Buffalo Bill State Historical Park.

Ogallala was the town at the end of the trail, where cowboys collected their paychecks after herding cattle north from Texas. After weeks of hot, dirty riding, the cowboys were ready to whoop it up in Ogallala. By 1885, the town had the reputation of being the wildest town in the Great Plains. Today it is better known for its location near Lake McConaughy, the largest lake in the state. Fishing, boating, sailboarding, and all kinds of other water sports are popular.

The two major highway routes west divide at Ogallala. U.S. Highway 26 follows the north branch of the Platte to Scottsbluff and into Wyoming, and Interstate 80 continues due west.

The Sand Hills

The Sand Hills cover more than half the state north of the Platte River. Very few towns appear on the maps of this region, and those few are extremely small. This is range country, where the ranches are huge.

Cherry County, in the northwestern part of the Sand Hills, is one of the largest counties in the United States. Yet only about

The sand hills of the
Valentine National
Wildlife Refuge

6,300 people live there, and nearly half of them are in the town of
Valentine. Many cities have more residents in a single block of
apartment houses than there are in Cherry County. Garden County
is much smaller than Cherry County, but even so, it covers more
square miles than the whole state of Rhode Island.

Although most of the land consists of sand dunes covered with
grass, there is a beauty to the landscape that is enchanting to those
who understand it. Soft hills roll away in endless processions to
meet a vast sky. Dozens of small lakes dot the western portion of
the Sand Hills. Several rivers and streams cross the region. Wildflowers add color to the grasses, and birds break the silence with
cheerful songs.

The Evelyn Sharp Airfield in Valley County is named for one of the nation's first female airmail pilots. Sharp was a flight instructor by age twenty and served as a fighter pilot during World War II. A display at the airport tells about her short but distinguished career, which ended in the crash of a P-38 when she was only twenty-four years old.

Custer County was once known as the Sod House Capital of the World. Because there were no trees to cut for lumber, early settlers made their homes out of sod. The thick, heavy sod of the prairies has been called Nebraska Marble. One sod house still exists near Comstock.

There are several wildlife refuges and two national forests in the Sand Hills. Established in 1902 by Theodore Roosevelt, Nebraska National Forest is the largest hand-planted forest in the country.

The Nebraska National Forest

The Panhandle

The Nebraska Panhandle is a squared-off area bordered by South Dakota, Wyoming, and Colorado. Interstate 80 crosses it in the south; the Platte River and U.S. Highway 26 make a northwesterly path through it to Scottsbluff and Wyoming. North of these main thoroughfares are plains, a pine ridge cut by canyons, and the lakes region of the Sand Hills.

Big Springs, just north of Interstate 80, was the site of a famous train robbery in 1877. An unusual memorial to the event has been

Visitors enjoy a few hours along the Oregon Trail Wagon Train.

erected near the railroad tracks: a carved wooden diorama of the train and of Sam Bass, the robber.

Ogallala had its wild cowboy days in the 1870s, but the town of Sidney was equally rough. Sidney was the principal rail shipping point for gold brought down from the Black Hills of South Dakota. Fortune hunters terrorized townspeople and railroad passengers. Robberies, murders, and lynchings were frequent. Sidney is a peaceful little town today.

Panorama Point, in the southwestern corner of the state, marks

Nebraska's highest elevation— 5,424 feet (1,653 m) above sea level. Views of the Rocky Mountains from the spot are spectacular.

Travelers heading west on U.S. Highway 26 will see the same important landmarks mentioned by the early pioneers: Courthouse Rock, Jail Rock, Chimney Rock, and Scotts Bluff. They can also relive part of the pioneer experience by taking a wagon ride of three hours or more on the Oregon Trail, near Bayard.

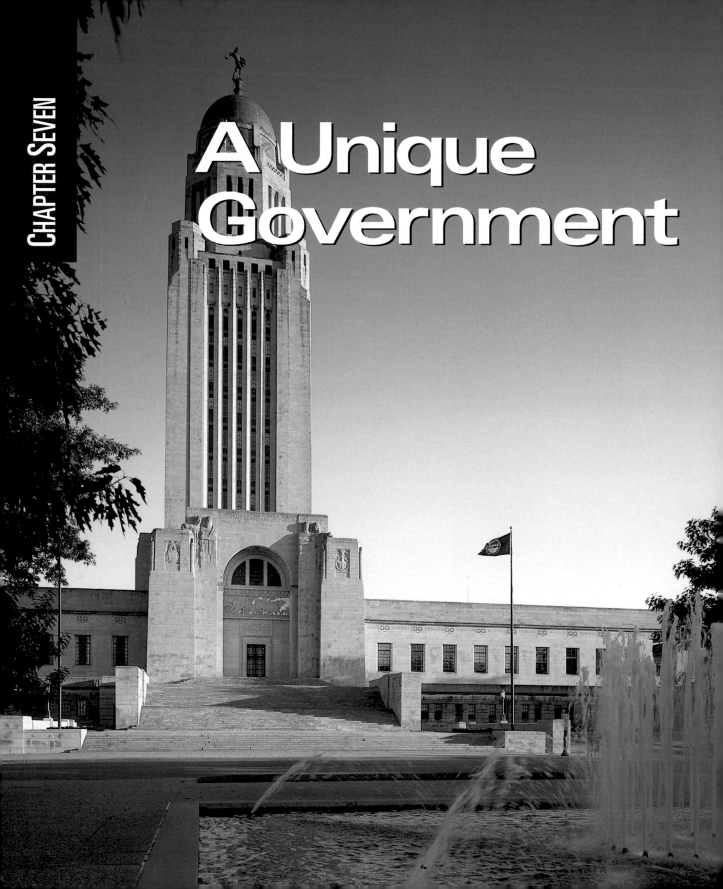

CHAPTER SEVEN

A Unique Government

Nebraska's state government is different from that of the other states. It has the same three branches: the executive, legislative, and judicial. However, instead of having a senate and a house of representatives, as the other states do, Nebraska has only a senate. This is called a unicameral legislature. Unicameral comes from a Latin word meaning "one chamber" or "one room." The forty-nine legislators in Nebraska are called state senators.

The interior of the state capitol

The Constitution

Nebraska became a state under a hastily written constitution submitted to the U.S. Congress in 1866. It was not satisfactory, however, and a new one was adopted in 1875. A constitutional convention met in 1920 and added a number of amendments to the document. Since then, 152 additional amendments have been adopted and made a part of the state's constitution.

The Executive Branch

Six officers of the state are elected by popular vote for four-year terms. They are the governor, lieutenant governor, secretary of state, auditor, treasurer, and attorney general. The governor and lieutenant governor are elected on a single ballot, representing the same

Opposite: The state capitol in Lincoln

The State Seal, Flag, and Motto

The Nebraska state seal, designed in 1867, includes several symbols of elements important to the settlement and growth of the new state. A blacksmith with a hammer and anvil represents the mechanical arts; sheaves of wheat, stalks of corn, and a settler's cabin are symbolic of agriculture; a steamboat and train are the means of transportation that brought people to the territory. In the background are the Rocky Mountains and above them, printed on a ribbon, is the motto "Equality Before the Law." A circular border reads "Great Seal of the State of Nebraska March 1st, 1867."

The state flag, which has flown since 1925, comprises the state seal on a field of blue. It was officially adopted by the legislature in 1963. ■

political party. Their terms of office are four years, and the officers may serve no more than two consecutive terms. Other officers and senators may run for reelection as many times as they wish.

Members of the Nebraska Board of Education, the Board of Regents of the University of Nebraska, and the Public Service Commission are also elected. Various state agencies do the work of the executive branch. The governor appoints the directors of these agencies. The other state officers have their own staffs.

The Unicameral Legislature

An amendment to the state constitution adopted in 1934 called for the formation of a one-house legislature, known as the Unicameral. The state was to be divided into at least thirty, but no more than fifty, legislative districts. There were forty-three districts in 1971; today there are forty-nine.

Nebraska's State Government

Executive Branch

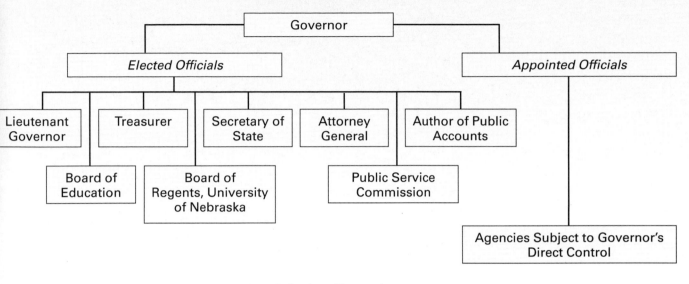

```
                            Governor
                 ┌─────────────┴─────────────┐
         Elected Officials              Appointed Officials
```

| Lieutenant Governor | Treasurer | Secretary of State | Attorney General | Author of Public Accounts |

Board of Education

Board of Regents, University of Nebraska

Public Service Commission

Agencies Subject to Governor's Direct Control

Legislative Branch

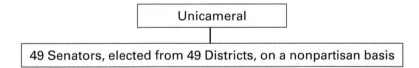

Unicameral

49 Senators, elected from 49 Districts, on a nonpartisan basis

Judicial Branch

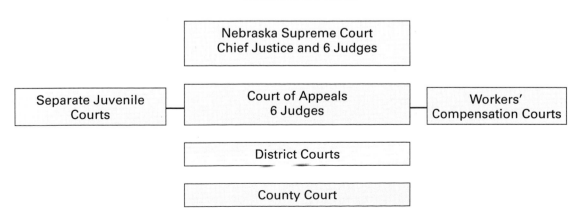

Nebraska Supreme Court
Chief Justice and 6 Judges

Separate Juvenile Courts

Court of Appeals
6 Judges

Workers' Compensation Courts

District Courts

County Court

Nebraska's Governors

Name	Party	Term
David Butler	Rep.	1867–1871
William H. James	Rep.	1871–1873
Robert W. Furnas	Rep.	1873–1875
Silas Garber	Rep.	1875–1879
Albinus Nance	Rep.	1879–1883
James W. Dawes	Rep.	1883–1887
John M. Thayer	Rep.	1887–1892
James E. Boyd	Dem.	1892–1893
Lorenzo Crounse	Rep.	1893–1895
Silas A. Holcomb	Fusion	1895–1899
William A. Poynter	Fusion	1899–1901
Charles H. Dietrich	Rep.	1901
Ezra P. Savage	Rep.	1901–1903
John H. Mickey	Rep.	1903–1907
George L. Sheldon	Rep.	1907–1909
Ashton C. Shallenberger	Dem.	1909–1911
Chester H. Aldrich	Rep.	1911–1913
John H. Morehead	Dem.	1913–1917
Keith Neville	Dem.	1917–1919
Samuel R. McKelvie	Rep.	1919–1923
Charles W. Bryan	Dem.	1923–1925
Adam McMullen	Rep.	1925–1929
Arthur J. Weaver	Rep.	1929–1931
Charles W. Bryan	Dem.	1931–1935
Robert Leroy Cochran	Dem.	1935–1941
Dwight Griswold	Rep.	1941–1947
Val Peterson	Rep.	1947–1953
Robert B. Crosby	Rep.	1953–1955
Victor E. Anderson	Rep.	1955–1959
Ralph G. Brooks	Dem.	1959–1960
Dwight W. Burney	Rep.	1960–1961
Frank B. Morrison	Dem.	1961–1967
Norbert T. Tiemann	Rep.	1967–1971
J. James Exon	Dem.	1971–1979
Charles Thone	Rep.	1979–1983
Robert Kerrey	Dem.	1983–1987
Kay A. Orr	Rep.	1987–1991
E. Benjamin Nelson	Dem.	1991–1999
Mike Johanns	Rep.	1999–

Nebraska's legislative chamber

Senators are elected to four-year terms on a nonpartisan basis—that is, without political-party affiliation. Elections are staggered, so that half the members are elected (or reelected) every two years. This system prevents any one election from creating a complete change of membership.

Champion for the Single Chamber

Nebraska elects two senators and three representatives to serve in the U.S. Congress. George W. Norris, born in Ohio in 1861, represented his state in the House of Representatives for ten years and in the Senate for thirty.

As a young man, Norris taught school to earn enough to get a college education and a law degree. From 1895 to 1902, he served as a district judge in Nebraska. He then decided to run for Congress on the Republican ticket. He had no idea he would be in Washington for so many years and would have so much influence on his state and the country. He intended to retire in 1936, but the voters persuaded him to run for another term as an Independent. He was reelected for a fifth term.

Norris had always been independent in spirit. He supported Democrats Al Smith and Franklin Delano Roosevelt in presidential elections. He worked hard for laws to provide farm relief and to protect the rights of workers to join unions. He fought for the Rural Electrification Act, which brought electricity to farmers all over the country.

Nationally, Senator Norris is best remembered for his long, hard struggle to establish the Tennessee Valley Authority (TVA). Over the years, this government corporation achieved its goals of controlling floods, making affordable electric power available, conserving natural resources, and creating recreational facilities. The TVA established thirty-nine dams. The first one, in eastern Tennessee, was named Norris Dam in honor of the Nebraska senator. The town of Norris, also named for him, was built nearby.

In Nebraska, Senator Norris is remembered best as the man who successfully campaigned for a constitutional amendment to establish a unicameral legislature. Other Nebraskans had been working on the idea since 1915. In 1934, Senator Norris took an active part in pushing it. He argued that it would be more efficient and less costly to have one legislative house. The senator's enormous popularity helped carry the day. Voters approved the amendment by a 60-percent majority. ■

How a Bill Becomes a Law

New laws are proposed as bills by senators. A committee of the Unicameral considers the bill and holds a hearing. Citizens may appear at the hearing and argue for or against the bill. Then the committee votes, either to kill the bill or refer it to the entire legislature. If the bill is passed, it is submitted to the governor. He or she has three choices: to sign it, to let it become law without his or her signature, or to veto it.

The Judicial Branch

Nebraska's supreme court consists of a chief justice and six judges, appointed by the governor. The six judges are chosen from regional lists. Below the supreme court is the court of appeals, also with six judges appointed by the governor and selected from the same regions as the supreme court judges.

All judges serve six-year terms and are appointed on a nonpartisan basis. At the next level are twelve district courts and separate juvenile and workers' compensation courts.

Nebraska's supreme court chamber

Nebraska's Capitol and Hall of Fame

Nebraska's state capitol towers over the city of Lincoln. It is an outstanding example of modern architecture. The central tower is 400 feet (122 m) tall. On a clear day, it can be seen from many miles away. On top of the tower is a gold-glazed, tiled dome. On top of the dome is the bronze figure of *The Sower* (above).

The capitol's paintings, carvings, and sculptures illustrate aspects of Nebraska's society and natural resources. Sculpted panels on the exterior wall represent the spirit of law in Western civilization from ancient to modern times. Interior and exterior decorations depict the importance of agriculture to the state, especially corn and wheat production.

Busts of noted Nebraskan men and women are mounted in the corridors. This section of the capitol is the Nebraska Hall of Fame. Every two years, a commission appointed by the governor nominates a person to be honored. In 1976, the U.S. bicentennial year, four nominees were selected.

The people in Nebraska's Hall of Fame represent a wide variety of occupations and achievements. Among the public servants honored are three-term governor and U.S. senator Dwight P. Griswold; Governor Robert W. Furnas, "the state's outstanding agricultural spokesman"; military hero General John J. Pershing; and U.S. senator George W. Norris, who promoted Nebraska's unicameral legislature and is considered the father of the Tennessee Valley Authority. Busts of poets John G. Neihardt and Loren Eiseley are on display, along with those of novelists Willa Cather, Bess Streeter Aldrich, and Mari Sandoz.

Father Edward J. Flanagan, founder of Boys Town, and Grace Abbott, a social worker who promoted legislation for the welfare of children and mothers, are remembered for their contributions to society. J. Sterling Morton and Nathan Roscoe Pound, who helped arouse public concern about the environment, are also represented, as are the Ponca chief Standing Bear and Susette LaFlesche Tibbles, champions of Indian rights.

Alongside these authors, poets, and public servants are some of Nebraska's one-of-a-kind individuals, such as soldier, buffalo hunter, and entertainer William "Buffalo Bill" Cody and livestock auctioneer Arthur Weimar Thompson, who was interested in modern methods of animal husbandry. ■

The Trial of Standing Bear

The U.S. government committed many acts of cruelty and persecution against the Native Americans in the West. Among these was forcing the Ponca people to relocate from their home in Nebraska to what is now Oklahoma, 500 miles (800 km) south, where one-third of the people died during the first year.

One of those who died was the son of the Ponca chief Standing Bear. The chief promised his son that he would take him back to their homeland to be buried. The government had ordered the Ponca to stay out of Nebraska, but the chief and a few of his people disobeyed the orders and walked the long distance back to their ancestral home. The government found out what they were doing and sent soldiers to arrest Standing Bear.

When they learned that Standing Bear was in prison, an Omaha newspaperman and two lawyers filed a suit in federal court seeking his freedom. The court sided with the chief and stated in a landmark ruling that "an Indian is a person within the meaning of the law." This ruling was an official declaration that all Native Americans are protected by the U.S. Constitution. ■

Local and Tribal Governments

Local government in Nebraska is run at the county and municipal levels. There are ninety-three counties. Sixty-six are governed by an elected board of commissioners; the rest by an elected board of supervisors.

In Nebraska, four sovereign groups of Native Americans—the Omaha, Ponca, Santee Sioux, and Winnebago—operate their own democratic form of government, headed by elected tribal councils.

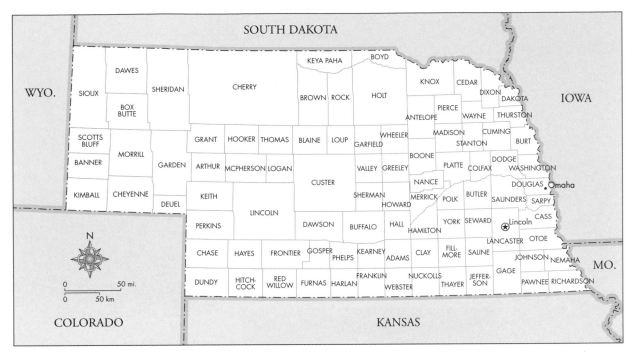

Nebraska's counties

Nebraska's State Song
"Beautiful Nebraska"

Music by Jim Fras; Words by Jim Fras and Guy G. Miller

Nebraska legislators discussed the selection of a state song through several sessions. They finally selected "Beautiful Nebraska," which was composed by Jim Fras of Lincoln. Fras, a Russian refugee who came to Lincoln in 1952, is a professional entertainer and composer. The song became the state's official song on June 21, 1967.

Beautiful Nebraska, peaceful prairieland,
Laced with many rivers and the hills of sand;
Dark green valleys cradled in the earth,
Rain and sunshine bring abundant birth.

(Chorus)
Beautiful Nebraska, as you look around,

You will find a rainbow reaching to the ground;
All these wonders by the Master's hand,
Beautiful Nebraskaland.

We are so proud of this state where we live.
There is no place that has so much to give.

(Repeat Chorus)

Nebraska's State Symbols

State nickname: Cornhusker State The Nebraska legislature started choosing state symbols in 1895. In honor of J. Sterling Morton, who founded Arbor Day, the Tree Planters' State was chosen as the state's official nickname. In 1945, a legislative act substituted the more commonly used nickname the Cornhusker State. This nickname refers to the fact that corn was husked by hand before laborsaving machinery was invented.

State bird: Western meadowlark The western meadowlark (above) was named the state bird in 1928. Five birds were listed on ballots sent to schools, and children voted for their favorites. They selected the western meadowlark, which is known for its joyful song.

State tree: Cottonwood The American elm was named the state tree in 1937. In the years following that decision, however, Dutch elm disease killed great numbers of Nebraskan elms. So in 1972 the cottonwood (above), often associated with pioneer Nebraska, replaced the elm as the state tree.

State gem: Blue agate This gemstone was made the official state gem on March 1, 1967, as part of the state's centennial celebration.

State fossil: Mammoth Large numbers of mammoth fossils have been uncovered in Nebraska. The remains of the long-extinct mammal have been found in nearly every county in the state.

State rock: Prairie agate The prairie agate was made the official state rock in 1967.

State grass: Little bluestem The little bluestem (right), a strong prairie grass, is an important native grass used for hay and forage. It was designated as the official state grass of Nebraska in 1969.

State insect: Honeybee Schoolchildren from Auburn, Nebraska, suggested that the honeybee should be the state insect because of its importance as a producer of honey and pollinator of crops since the days of early settlement. The legislature made the children's choice official in 1974.

State mammal: White-tailed deer In 1981, the white-tailed deer became the state mammal.

State poet laureate: John G. Neihardt The 1921 legislature named John G. Neihardt as the poet laureate of Nebraska. He wrote five long narrative poems that are regarded as national epics. The legislative resolution said, in part, that his work "inspired in Americans the love of the land and its heroes whereby great national traditions are built and perpetuated." The title belongs permanently to Neihardt.

State poet: William Kloefkorn William Kloefkorn of Lincoln was proclaimed Nebraska's first state poet on September 11, 1982. Kloefkorn, a university professor, has written many poems and books about prairie life. He was one of the founders of Nebraska's Poets-in-the-Schools program.

State flower: Goldenrod On April 4, 1895, the day the state's first nickname became official, a law was signed designating the goldenrod as the state flower. An article published at the time said of the goldenrod: "It is a native, and only a true native should be our representative. It has a long season, and nothing could better represent the hardy endurance of Nebraska's pioneers." ■

Making a Living

From sodbusting to high tech—that's the story of Nebraska during the past 100 years. At the beginning of the twentieth century, Nebraskans were living in sod houses and working the land with horse-drawn plows. By the end of the century, Nebraska had become a leader in the worldwide industry of telecommunications. More schoolchildren in the state are learning how to surf the Internet than how to drive a tractor.

Agriculture

Agriculture and food processing are very important to the economy of the state and the nation. About 95 percent of the land in Nebraska is used for farming or ranching. Nebraska's farmers and ranchers produce enough grain and meat to feed millions of people.

Modern methods of soil conservation and irrigation have made it possible to produce more crops than ever with fewer workers. A generation ago, most people would have stayed on their farms or

Opposite: Herding cattle is one way to make a living in Nebraska.

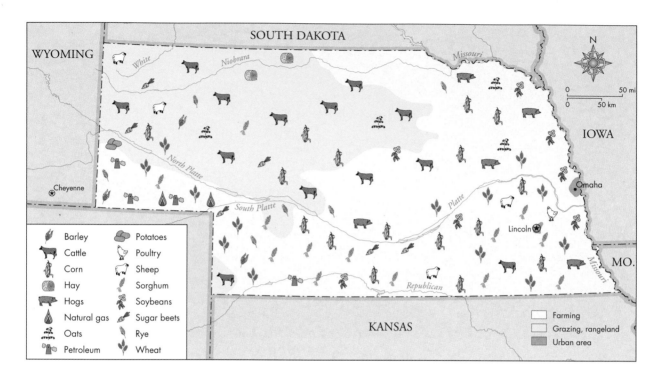

Nebraska's natural resources

ranches; today, they work in offices, stores, and factories in the cities.

Corn, wheat, grain sorghum, soybeans, rye, oats, and sugar beets are among the major crops grown in Nebraska. Corn is the top cash crop. Nebraska is the nation's leading producer of alfalfa meal and of Great Northern beans.

What Nebraska Grows, Manufactures, and Mines

Agriculture	Manufacturing	Mining
Beef cattle	Food products and food processing	Sand
Hogs		Stone
Corn	Machinery	Potash
Wheat	Instruments and related products	
Grain sorghum		
Soybeans		

How to Broil a Perfect Steak

Nebraska is world renowned for its beef production. Cooking steaks, however, is not always as easy as it seems. Here is an easy way to broil a perfect steak.

Always thaw steak in the refrigerator. Cold temperatures discourage the growth of bacteria, reducing the risk of food poisoning. Always wash your hands before and after handling raw meat.

Place the thawed steaks on a pan 2 inches from the broiler. The steak should be turned once so that it cooks on both sides. Always use tongs to turn the meat over; piercing the meat with a fork causes the natural juices to run out.

A steak $1/2$ inch to 1 inch thick should be cooked for five minutes on one side and four minutes on the other for rare meat; seven minutes on one side and five on the other for medium-rare meat; and ten minutes on one side and eight on the other for well-done meat.

Millions of cattle graze where the buffalo once roamed. Large feedlots in various locations prepare livestock for market. Hogs, lambs, and poultry are also raised in the state.

The processing of meats and other foods is a large industry that depends on Nebraska's farms and ranches. The Omaha plant of Campbell Soup Company produces more than two hundred frozen food products that are shipped all over North America. Swanson TV dinners were first produced in Omaha.

Other industries depend directly on agriculture, too. These include the making of pharmaceuticals, farm equipment and buildings, and irrigation systems.

Industry has become as important as farming to the Nebraskan way of life.

Mining and Manufacturing

Mining is not a huge part of Nebraska's economy, but there are some deposits of sand, gravel, stone, potash, and other nonmineral elements. The southwestern part of the state and the southern Panhandle have some oil and natural gas.

After food processing, the main products manufactured in Nebraska are industrial, transportation, and agricultural machinery and equipment, as well as electronic and other electrical equipment. Printing and publishing are also important. Most of the manufacturing is based in the eastern part of the state.

Transportation and Utilities

Nebraska is located in the center of the United States. This strategic position gives the state quick and easy access to all other parts of the country.

Interstate 80 is the nation's most heavily traveled route across the continent. The largest cities of Nebraska are served by major airlines, and there are more than one hundred municipal and commercial airports in the

Grand Island Airport is among many municipal and commercial terminals in the state.

state. Eight ports on the Missouri River have regular barge service. Rail service is provided by Union Pacific, the nation's largest railroad system; by Burlington Northern; and by Chicago and Northwestern. Amtrak serves passengers in five communities.

The Company That Sells Fun

For more than sixty years, Omaha's Oriental Trading Company has been selling stuff that makes you say "Hey, I had one of these when I was a kid," according to the company's president Terry Watanabe (right). For example, among the many low-priced toys and novelties carried by the company are Chinese finger traps and the Slinky.

Watanabe began working at his father's company when he was six years old. He became the company's president at age twenty. The "company that sells fun" has grown to a business that employs 3,000 people. ■

Nebraska has the only public power system in the United States, which results in electric rates as much as 14 percent lower than the national average.

Nebraska at Work

As the twentieth century draws to a close, the economy looks good in Nebraska. The unemployment rate is only about half that of the national average. The people who do not work at agricultural jobs work in the following industries:

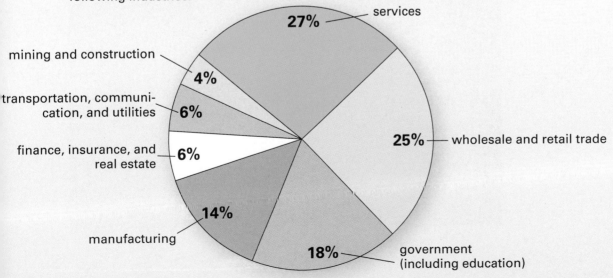

- services 27%
- wholesale and retail trade 25%
- government (including education) 18%
- manufacturing 14%
- finance, insurance, and real estate 6%
- transportation, communication, and utilities 6%
- mining and construction 4%

Telecommunications

Nearly two-thirds of the people in Nebraska live within 50 miles (80 km) of Omaha. Once known primarily as a meat-packing center, Omaha is highly diversified today. It has experienced a steady growth in size and number of businesses during the past fifty years. Omaha is a major center for telecommunications.

Much of Omaha's phenomenal success in moving into modern high-tech industries is a result of the influence of its neighbor, the U.S. Strategic Command (formerly called SAC, now known as STRATCOM), headquartered at Offut Air Force Base in Bellevue. During the Cold War, the U.S. military developed a huge and complex system of telecommunications. In fact, the system was much larger than was needed for government use, so it was made available to civilians in the 1980s.

The Offut Air Force Base in Bellevue

SITEL Corporation

SITEL, located in Omaha, is one of dozens of telecommunications companies in Nebraska. "Actually, our business is teleservicing," says Jim Lynch, founder and chairman of the board. By "teleservicing," he means that his company performs services for other companies—just about any type of service that requires a telephone and a computer.

And that's just what you would see if you were to visit a SITEL office (right)—rows of people sitting at desks, each with a telephone and a computer. The business works like this: For example, let's say that your father wants to buy insurance from a company that is a client of SITEL. He dials the company's phone number. A SITEL operator in Omaha answers the phone, even though the insurance company is located in Connecticut. The operator's computer is hooked up to the insurance company's main computer, so the SITEL operator can answer your father's questions in seconds.

"The phenomenal growth in the speed of transmitting information is the reason companies like ours have been so successful," says Lynch. "Our employees handle more than thirteen million calls a month."

SITEL has offices in several small buildings in different parts of Omaha. There are also regional offices in several other countries. The company provides services all over the world, in thirty different languages. ■

At the time, Omaha was already a communications center. Northwestern Bell had a large workforce that was well trained in telecommunications. Western Electric/AT&T employed many workers skilled in manufacturing equipment for the industry. Omaha was in the right place at the right time—and it had the right people—to get into a new and growing field. Today, more than 50,000 people in Nebraska are employed by nearly a thousand companies in information-related businesses.

Rose Blumkin, Entrepreneur

Known as Mrs. B to thousands of shoppers, Rose Blumkin's life is a great story about a poor immigrant girl who started a multimillion-dollar business.

Mrs. B came to Omaha from Russia as a young woman, married, and raised a family. During the Great Depression of the 1930s, the family needed extra money. Mrs. B opened a pawnshop, which she gradually expanded into a small furniture store. Even though the business was close to bankruptcy at one time, over the years it grew into the gigantic Nebraska Furniture Mart, which occupies several city blocks in Omaha.

"Sell cheap, tell the truth, don't cheat, and don't take kickbacks," was Mrs. B's creed. Even as the store grew larger, she stayed directly involved in managing it. People tell stories of seeing her in the store, scooting around on a golf cart, talking to customers. They remember that she often offered special bargains to newly-weds.

When Mrs. B was nearly one hundred years old, she sold her business for $55 million. Her reputation was so honorable, the buyer did not ask for an inventory or an audit. "She gave us her word," he explained, and that was good enough. Rose Blumkin died in 1998 at age 104. ■

The industry expanded rapidly in the 1960s when toll-free 800 numbers became available for public use. Suddenly, many operators were needed to answer calls for information and service. New companies sprang up in Omaha, often in the basements of people's homes. An entrepreneur would install a few telephone lines, hire a few part-time employees, and, before long, his or her business was growing by leaps and bounds. Soon, Omaha was the "800 capital of the world."

These successes spun off new manufacturers of telecommunications equipment. That new industry meant more jobs. Then, local trade schools and colleges began to develop courses to train potential employees to make and service the phones, computers, cables, and other equipment. The need for training again created jobs.

Telemarketing is one aspect of telecommunications. Insurance companies, credit card companies, and other businesses that rely on a huge volume of telephone sales depend on several Omaha companies to handle many of their telemarketing services to customers. There are two types of telemarketing: inbound and outbound. Inbound telemarketing requires answering calls about products or services. For example, when a product is advertised on television, there is often an 800 number to call to order the product. The people who receive the calls are providing inbound telemarketing services. Outbound telemarketing consists of calls to customers to solicit new sales.

CHAPTER NINE

The Many Faces of Nebraska

Some of Nebraska's settlers came from states to the east, but many more came from Europe. Immigrants were lured by the prospect of free land offered through the Homestead Act. They came from Germany, Sweden, Denmark, Bohemia, Russia, Poland, France, Ireland, England, and Italy. By 1900, 15 percent of the population of the state were of German heritage.

After railroads had been built across the country, the pace of immigration speeded up greatly. The railroad companies helped to develop communities along their routes and actively recruited new settlers from abroad in order to boost sales of their lands. Group settlements were encouraged. In 1869 and 1870, the Union Pacific brought a group of Swedish people to Saunders and Polk Counties. Sixty families from Nova Scotia settled in Colfax County. A group of German-born people who had been living in Russia traveled to Lincoln on the Burlington Railroad.

The Union Pacific Railroad transported a group of Swedish settlers to Nebraska in 1869 and 1870.

Opposite: An afternoon at the Winnebago Pow-wow

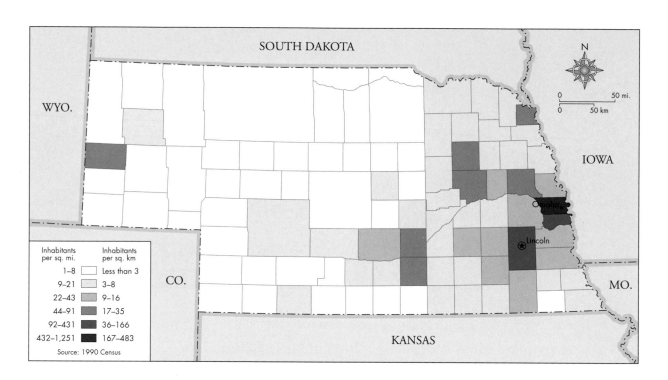

Nebraska's population density

SOUTH DAKOTA

WYO.

IOWA

Omaha

Lincoln

Inhabitants per sq. mi.	Inhabitants per sq. km
1–8	Less than 3
9–21	3–8
22–43	9–16
44–91	17–35
92–431	36–166
432–1,251	167–483

Source: 1990 Census

CO.

KANSAS

MO.

A few African-Americans moved to Nebraska after the end of the Civil War. Some tried homesteading; more went to the cities. According to the census, there were 6,269 blacks in the state in 1900. Omaha's black population doubled between 1910 and 1920. The population of Nebraska has grown steadily in every decade, except during the years of the Great Depression in the 1930s.

Nebraskans Today

In 1996, Nebraska's total population was estimated at 1,652,093. Half the people lived in the metropolitan areas of Omaha and Lincoln; four out of five lived in the eastern third of the state. According to the 1990 census, the main ethnic groups were German, Irish, English, Czech, Swedish, Polish, and Danish. African-Americans made up 3.64 percent of the total; Native Americans and Asians each represented 0.79 percent. Most residents—70 percent—were born in Nebraska, 16 percent in other Midwestern states. Roman Catholics comprised the largest religious group; among Protestant groups, the Lutheran Church had the most members.

In 1990, more than nine out of ten Nebraskans were identified as Caucasian, although the population has become more diverse. In recent years, the percentages of African-Americans, Native Americans, Asians, and Hispanics have increased. At the same time, the rural population has decreased and the urban population has grown.

Even though most people living in Nebraska were born in the United States, many residents still celebrate their ethnic heritages.

Population of Nebraska's Major Cities (1990)

Omaha	335,795
Lincoln	191,972
Grand Island	39,386
Bellevue	30,982
Kearney	24,396
Fremont	23,680

The annual Czech festival at Wilber

The town of O'Neill calls itself the Irish Capital of Nebraska, and St. Patrick's Day is enthusiastically celebrated there each year. The town of Wilber, known as the National Czech Capital, celebrates an annual Czech Festival. A Czech museum and the Czech foods served at the Wilber Hotel are reminders of where some of the town's early settlers came from.

Other popular ethnic festivals held annually in Nebraska are Germanfest in Syracuse, the Swedish festival in Stromsburg, and the Danish festival in Dannebrog. The American Historical Society of Germans from Russia is a very active organization in Lincoln.

Native Americans

The Native Americans living in Nebraska today represent the Pawnee, Omaha, Oto, Ponca, Santee Sioux, Dakota Sioux, Cheyenne, Potawatomi, Arapaho, Sac, and Fox. Many of these people live on the three reservations in the state: Omaha, Winnebago, and Santee Sioux. They lead modern lives, farming or working in other jobs. Tribal councils govern local affairs.

Native American children attend public schools. Traditional arts, crafts, and ceremonial observances are encouraged. Annual powwows in Santee, Winnebago, Pine Ridge (South Dakota), Niobrara, and Macy celebrate American Indian rituals and traditions.

Ranch Life

Farming and ranching are the major occupations of the people in the rural areas of Nebraska. People often wonder why western Nebraska ranches are so large. The reason is the vegetation of the

Ranchers still love the wide-open spaces, but often they travel by truck rather than on horseback.

Sand Hills. The prairie grasses there are highly nutritious for cattle, but they are also fragile and easily destroyed by erosion or overgrazing. Good ranch management requires a range of 10 to 15 acres (4 to 6 ha) for each bull and each cow with a calf—even more in some areas. Horses eat twice as much grass. So a ranch with 500 head of cattle needs 5,000 to 7,500 acres (2,025 to 3,035 ha) of grassland, plus some more for the horses.

Cowboys used to live a very different life from farmers and townspeople, spending more time with animals than with other people. Modern technology—access to television, cellular telephones, computers, and other devices—has lessened the differences between everyday urban and ranch life. But it is still a long drive from most ranches into town, and ranchers and cowboys are still accustomed to wide-open spaces.

Cowboy Lingo

In movies, cowboys have a colorful language, sprinkled with words borrowed from Native Americans and the Spanish *vaqueros* (cow herders) of the Southwest and Mexico. Some of the following words are no longer in common use. Others are standard ranch terms.

Brand   A mark on an animal made with a hot iron to identify the owner

Bronco   A small, lively horse (from the Spanish word meaning "wild")

Bulldogging   Throwing a steer by grabbing its horns and turning its head

Cayuse   A pony; originally meant an Indian pony, from the name of a tribe

Chaparajos   Leather overalls or leggings, usually called chaps (from Spanish)

Chaparral   Dense growth of brush or small trees (from Spanish)

Chow   Food, also called grub, chuck, and eats

Corral   A fenced enclosure for animals (from Spanish)

Dogies   Young steers; originally orphaned steers

Hog-tied   A calf that cannot stand because three legs have been tied together

Horse wrangler   A person who keeps horses for other riders

Lariat   English version of the Spanish word *la reata,* "the rope"

Maverick   A stray animal without a brand

Pinto   A spotted horse (from the Spanish word meaning "painted")

Rodeo   A show where cowboys compete in roping and riding (below)

Roundup   The gathering together of a herd of cattle (left)

Tenderfoot   A greenhorn, or newcomer; originally referred to eastern cattle that were shipped west

Vaquero   Cow herder (from Spanish)

Wrassle   Variation of the word *wrestle* ■

Schools and Libraries

Nebraska's first school was established at Fort Atkinson in the 1820s. The small community also had a library. Free public school education was provided for all children in the state when the constitution was adopted in 1875.

Attendance at school is mandatory for those from seven to sixteen years of

Nebraska's educational system has changed dramatically since this one-room schoolhouse was built in Otoe County.

age. As of 1996, there were 668 public school districts in the state, as well as some private schools. Education in Nebraska is supervised by a nonpartisan state board of education.

Schools are far apart in some of the less populated sections of the state. Some parents choose to educate their children at home. Others send them to private or parochial boarding schools. Some mothers live in town with their children during the school week, returning to their ranches only on weekends. Sometimes children board with families who live closer to the schools.

The University of Nebraska has campuses at Lincoln, Omaha, Kearney, and Curtis. The state also supports state colleges at Chadron, Peru, and Wayne, in addition to a statewide community college system. In addition, there are more than twenty private colleges in Nebraska.

There are two tribally controlled colleges for Native Americans in Nebraska. Little Priest Tribal College, near Winnebago, teaches native language and culture along with other academic programs. Associate of arts and associate of science degrees are offered, as are certificate programs in early childhood education and computer information systems. Nebraska Indian Community College, chartered and organized by the Omaha, Santee Sioux, and Winnebago tribes, has campuses in Macy and Niobrara. Both vocational/technical and academic transfer programs are offered.

The first public library in the state was started in Omaha

Children read books and work on computers in the Omaha Public Library.

in 1871. A few years later, the legislature authorized a system of free public libraries and reading rooms throughout the state. Today the state's hundreds of public, school, and special libraries share their resources through a network supported by a state library commission.

Febold Feboldson

Gothenburg, Nebraska, was the home of Febold Feboldson. Like Antoine Barada, Feboldson was a man who possessed superhuman strength—but unlike Barada, he was a fictitious character. Many people published stories about him. One writer suggested that Feboldson was a Swedish lumberjack who worked for the legendary lumberjack Paul Bunyan in the woods of the North, then came to Nebraska to work on his own. Because there were no trees for him to cut in Nebraska, he instead wrestled with tornadoes, droughts, hostile natives, politicians, and disease. ■

Famous Nebraskans

Nebraska has been home to many Americans who have made their mark on society and the world. Some were born in the state; some achieved their prominence after moving into the state. Many of these people are honored in the Nebraska Hall of Fame.

One Nebraska native rose to the highest political office in the world—U.S. president Gerald R. Ford. Nebraska has also produced three Nobel Prize laureates: George Beadle for science, awarded in 1958; Val L. Fitch for physics in 1980; and Lawrence Klein for economics in 1980.

George Beadle, winner of the 1958 Nobel Prize for science

Summer on a Cattle Ranch

"Mamma, tell me what it was like when you lived on the ranch," begged Tom.

"Oh, you've heard all my stories a thousand times," Tom's mother, Anna, protested. But it never took much persuasion to get her to talk about her childhood. Now, the family lived a thousand miles away from the cattle spread in the Nebraska Panhandle where she grew up.

"Tell me about the horses."

"Okay. Well, my dad or mother started carrying me with them on horseback by the time I could walk. Then, at four or five, they'd hold the reins and walk the horse around with me on his back. I really can't remember when I started riding alone."

"Was it your very own horse?"

"Oh, yes, I always had my own. At first, it was a huge draft horse, because they're the gentlest kind. I really wanted a prettier, sleeker one, but I had to wait until I was a really good rider."

Anna told how she began helping to "wrassle" (wrestle) calves before she was old enough to go to school. This was how the children helped with branding. Each ranch has its own brand, a special shape or monogram, that identifies the ownership in case an animal strays away from the herd.

The whole family got into the act. Her dad would throw his rope around the hind legs of the calf and drag it to where one of the ranch hands was waiting with a hot branding iron. Then, Anna and her mom and brother all held the calf as still as they could while the brand was burned into its hide. Of course it hurt the calf, but not for very long. It's quite a job to hold the struggling creature still for a minute or so, until the job is done.

Whenever the cattle had to be moved from one grazing place to another, the children rode along to help keep the herd together. Water for the animals was pumped by windmills (above) dotted all over the ranch. Several thousand cattle were spread out over several locations. On hot days, the cattle would bunch together near a windmill, for water and possibly a bit of shade. Anna's father sometimes asked her to ride out with him to check the herd and make sure everything was all right. "That was a really boring job," she told Tom. "All we did was ride from windmill to windmill, all day long in the hot sun."

People are really spread out in ranch country. Anna's nearest playmates lived 10 miles (16 km) away. But they got together, either by horseback or by pickup truck, which most of the kids were able to drive on the ranch roads by the time they were tall enough to reach the pedals.

There wasn't much in the way of entertainment, either. Children had to make their own fun. "We'd make up endless games with toy animals, pretending to be on a wagon train going west. We'd go rock climbing in the hills. Many times, we actually found fossils of prehistoric animals. We'd make mud pies and have mud fights and get so dirty we'd have to take long, hot baths to got rid of the barnyard smell.

"My brother and his best friend were always getting into mischief. There were some close calls, like the time they went swimming in a water tank and almost drowned. And another time, one of them climbed up on top of the windmill and fell off. One of the neighbors said,

'Every year when school lets out, I start praying that the boys manage to stay alive until fall!'"

The biggest social event of the season was branding time (above). All the neighbors would get together for a huge noontime dinner—there might be fifty or sixty people in all. The women would have been fixing food for days, maybe even weeks. There would be beef, chicken, and maybe ham. Always a lot of mashed potatoes and gravy, as well as two or three other kinds of potatoes; vegetables; several salads— molded jello salads, fruit salads, vegetable salads—homemade bread and rolls. And a huge selection of desserts—cakes and many different kinds of pie.

"Do you think it's still like that on the ranch these days, Mom?"

"Probably not too different for the kids. Home entertainment has changed some. Most families have TV by satellite dish, and they rent videos when they go to town.

"One big difference is that not many families raise their own chickens and pigs or grow big vegetable gardens any more. A lot of the mothers now have jobs, either full-time or part-time. So more things come from the store, instead of being raised at home. But ranch life still revolves around the cattle and the horses."

"When are you going to take me out there for a visit, Mom?" Tom begged, as he always did when she told him ranch stories. ■

CHAPTER TEN

Entertainment and Leisure Time

It's Saturday in Lincoln, a bright, warm autumn day. It reminds one of a poem written long ago that describes "October's bright blue weather." A huge roar rises over the walls of Memorial Stadium. The Cornhuskers must have made another brilliant play.

The University of Nebraska's famous football team, the Cornhuskers, always draws a crowd for its home games. All 76,000 seats of the stadium are filled—it has been sold out for more than two hundred consecutive home games.

Nebraskans are loyal supporters of the Cornhuskers, who have garnered five Big 8 Conference titles and several college bowl victories. The team defeated Miami at the 1995 Orange Bowl with a score of 24 to 17 and beat Florida with a huge margin of 62 to 24 at the Fiesta Bowl in 1996. The Cornhuskers were named national champions by the Associated Press (AP) poll in 1994 and 1995.

More Sports

Nebraskans take soccer seriously, too. The game is played all over the state by people of all ages—even preschoolers get into this act.

The University of Nebraska's football team, the Cornhuskers, usually draws sold-out crowds.

Opposite: Picking strawberries on a sunny Nebraska afternoon

The College World
Series is hosted in
Omaha each June.

The Lincoln Brigade Soccer Club plays ten outdoor home games at Seacrest Field and a full indoor season in winter at Pershing Auditorium. Team members come from the University of Nebraska and nearby colleges. Omaha has a soccer club, too. Nebraska has the nation's highest ratio of registered soccer players, in proportion to the population.

In Omaha, the biggest sports event of the year is in June, when the College World Series comes to town. About a quarter of a million people from all over the country follow their favorite teams to Rosenblatt Stadium. Omaha has hosted this event for fifty years. Omaha also has a professional AAA baseball team, the Royals, and a professional hockey team, the Lancers.

During the first weekend in May, some 2,000 runners convene in Lincoln for the Marathon and Half-Marathon races. These events have been held for twenty years. Omaha hosts the annual Riverfront Marathon.

Opposite: Omaha's
AAA baseball team,
the Royals

Nebraska's Big Rodeo is held in Burwell each July.

Other annual sports events in Lincoln include the regional championship meets in gymnastics and roller skating. Lincoln is the home of the National Museum of Roller Skating.

Cowboys and cowgirls demonstrate their skills in riding, roping, and steer wrestling at rodeos held in several Nebraska towns. North Platte hosts the famous Buffalo Bill Rodeo in June. Each July, lots of visitors arrive in Burwell, in the southeastern part of the Sand Hills, to watch Nebraska's Big Rodeo. The Old Cowboys and Cowgirls Rodeo in Hyannis is limited to contestants who are more than forty years of age. The World Championship Rodeo is held at Ak-Sar-Ben Field and Coliseum in Omaha each September.

Basketball and football are popular high school sports throughout the state. Teenagers and adults get together in local parks to play pickup softball. People of all ages fish, hunt, bicycle, ride horses, and cross-country ski.

Nebraska native Bob Gibson pitched the St. Louis Cardinals to many victories.

Max Baer, two-time heavyweight boxing champion

Sports Heroes

Perhaps it is not surprising, because Nebraskans are such loyal sports fans, that the state has produced several outstanding athletes. Grover Cleveland Alexander was a pitching star in the early days of Major League Baseball. Bob Gibson, another pitcher, led the St. Louis Cardinals to 251 victories. Max Baer was the world heavyweight boxing champion in 1934 and 1935.

Several Nebraskans have won Olympic medals: Gary Anderson for rifle shooting, Lewis Anderson for track and field; Jim Hartung for gymnastics, and H. C. Wittman for cycling.

Grover Cleveland Alexander

Grover Cleveland "Pete" Alexander (also called "Alexander the Great" by his fans) is still remembered as one of baseball's most successful pitchers. Born in Elba, Nebraska, in 1887, Alexander joined the Philadelphia Phillies when he was twenty-four years of age. In 1916, he set a record when he pitched sixteen shutouts (no-run games). He won thirty or more games in each of three consecutive years and led the National League in earned run average five times.

In 1926, Alexander pitched for the St. Louis Cardinals in three World Series games against the New York Yankees. The deciding game was a cliff-hanger. The bases were loaded, and there were two men out. Alexander was called in to save the situation. Without any warm-up, he went to the mound, struck the batter out, and won the series for the Cards. ■

Music, Drama, and Dance

The "lively arts" are very lively in Omaha and Lincoln. Omaha has twenty-four theaters, an opera company, a professional symphony orchestra, ballet troupe, children's theater, and youth orchestra. Each summer, the Nebraska Shakespeare Festival presents its special seasonal event, Shakespeare on the Green.

In spring, the Festival of American Folk Dance is held in Lincoln. This annual event, the oldest of its kind, has been presented for nearly sixty years. Each summer, Lincoln also hosts the International Thespian Festival. High school students from all over attend, along with parents, teachers, and representatives of college theater departments. Participants take part in workshops and perform in theater productions.

More than one hundred towns in Nebraska have one or more

active arts organizations. These may be arts councils, little theater companies, musical groups, or museums.

The Brownville Village Theater is an eight-week summer repertory theater. (A repertory theater presents the same group of actors in different plays during a season.) The Theatre of the American West, in Republican City, stages dramas, comedies, and musicals in what used to be a school gymnasium. People get together for a barbecue dinner before the performances. Casts include local and regional actors as well as members of the theater company.

Famous Entertainers

There must be something about the Nebraska air or the prairie grass that creates celebrities. For such a small state, Nebraska has produced a remarkable number of people who have achieved success and fame in the entertainment world.

Buffalo Bill Cody was the first nationally and internationally known entertainer from Nebraska, made famous by his popular Wild West shows. Harold Lloyd was a leading star in silent-

Marlon Brando

Marlon Brando was born in Omaha in 1924. During his career spanning more than fifty years, he has been recognized as one of America's greatest film actors.

Brando was nominated three times for an Academy Award before winning one for his role in *On the Waterfront* (1954). He was again awarded an Oscar for best actor for his performance as a crime boss in *The Godfather* (1972). This time, however, he refused to attend the ceremonies or accept the award. He told the world that his refusal of the honor was his act of protest against the treatment of Native Americans by the film industry. ■

Johnny Carson, long-time host of *The Tonight Show*, grew up in Nebraska.

Henry Fonda in the 1940 film version of John Steinbeck's novel *The Grapes of Wrath*

movie days. Darryl F. Zanuck, film producer and co-founder of 20th Century Fox movie studio, came from Wahoo. Johnny Carson and Dick Cavett, two of television's best-known talk-show hosts, both grew up in Nebraska.

Nebraska-born actor Henry Fonda received an Academy Award and a Tony Award, as did actress Sandy Dennis. Other movie and television actors from the Cornhusker State include Marlon Brando, Montgomery Clift, James Coburn, David Janssen, Swoosie Kurtz, Dorothy McGuire, Nick Nolte, Robert Taylor, and Irene Worth.

Literature

The talents of writers, editors, poets, and public speakers are appreciated in Nebraska. More than half the men and women who have been inducted into the state's Hall of Fame were known, at least partially,

Three Authors

Willa Cather (above) was born in Virginia in 1873, but she grew up in the Nebraska of pioneer days. A graduate of the University of Nebraska, Cather spent much of her adult life working in the East. Her historical novels, such as *O Pioneers!* and *My Antonia,* were based on her memories and knowledge of Nebraska. Her childhood home in Red Cloud—which was the setting for six of her twelve novels—is a state historic site, open to the public. Cather won a Pulitzer Prize in 1923 for *One of Ours.*

Bess Streeter Aldrich (right) was born in Iowa in 1881. After finishing college and teaching for a few years, she married and moved to Elmwood, Nebraska.

Aldrich was the author of nearly a dozen novels, most of them describing pioneer family life in Iowa and Nebraska. More than 160 of her short stories have been published. One of her best-known books is *A Lantern in Her Hand.* The University of Nebraska awarded Aldrich with an honorary doctor of letters degree. Her home in Elmwood is open to visitors. The Bess Streeter Aldrich Museum is located in the Elmwood Library.

The novels by Cather and Aldrich describes the lives of early homesteaders and farmers in eastern Nebraska. Mari Sandoz (above, right) lived in and wrote about the upper Niobrara region of the Sand Hills. She wrote about real people,

but told their stories as if they were fictional characters. Her first and most famous book, *Old Jules,* was about her father. It is considered to be her masterpiece. She began gathering material for the book in 1920. It was not finally accepted for publication until 1935, after rejections from thirteen publishers. Each time it was turned down, Sandoz edited, cut, and revised the manuscript. Sandoz continued to write for the rest of her life and published more than a dozen books about pioneers and Native Americans.

Cather, Aldrich, and Sandoz have all been inducted into the Nebraska Hall of Fame in Lincoln. ■

A Museum without Walls

A "sculpture garden" stretches across the state of Nebraska. Nine works are on display at rest areas along Interstate 80. The idea for the statewide outdoor exhibit was conceived as part of the celebration of the American Revolution Bicentennial. Arts councils and businesses in the state raised most of the funds to finance the project. The pieces on display interpret aspects of Nebraska life and history. ■

because of their ability to communicate. J. Sterling Morton, noted for his work in agriculture, was also a newspaperman. The nationally famous orator and politician William Jennings Bryan was an editor and author of many articles and books.

Pioneer life in Nebraska fascinated three women who studied it and wrote about it: Willa Cather, Bess Streeter Aldrich, and Mari Sandoz. All these women achieved fame as authors while they were still alive.

Museums

The Joslyn Art Museum in Omaha and the University of Nebraska Art Galleries in Lincoln are the premier art museums in Nebraska. Artwork from around the world, spanning the past 2,000 years, is on display at the Joslyn. There is also an excellent collection of American Western art.

The university's galleries include a collection of twentieth-century American art and a sculpture garden. The well-known painters Frederic Remington (1861–1909) and Charles M. Russell (1864–1926) are represented in a collection of Great Plains art. The University of Nebraska State Museum, located in Morrill Hall, has one of the nation's largest collection of fossils, as well as rocks, minerals, and Native American exhibits.

The Museum of Nebraska Art (MONA) in Kearney specializes in works by Nebraska artists as well as other artwork with Nebraska themes. Housed in Kearney's elegant old post office, built in 1911, are twelve exhibition galleries. There is also a sculpture garden on the grounds.

Nebraska went from its pioneer days into the age of cyberspace in fewer than two hundred years. Who knows what adventures lie ahead? Nebraska's human achievements have been remarkable. Equally remarkable, however, are the state's natural wonders, which outlive generations after generations of people—the vast expanses of waving prairie grass; the big sky stretching to infinity; the rivers and lakes, sand hills and valleys; and the awe-inspiring sight of thousands of sandhill cranes returning to visit, year after year.

The University of Nebraska Art Galleries in Lincoln houses one of the state's many excellent art collections.

Timeline

United States History

The first permanent British settlement is established in North America at Jamestown. **1607**

Pilgrims found Plymouth Colony, the second permanent British settlement. **1620**

America declares its independence from England. **1776**

The Treaty of Paris officially ends the Revolutionary War in America. **1783**

The U.S. Constitution is written. **1787**

Louisiana Purchase almost doubles the size of the United States. **1803**

United States and Britain **1812–15** fight the War of 1812.

The North and South fight **1861–65** each other in the American Civil War.

Nebraska State History

1682 René-Robert Cavelier, Sieur de La Salle, claims the region drained by the Mississippi River, including present-day Nebraska, for France.

1720 The Pawnee defeat Spanish forces led by Pedro de Villasur along the Platte River.

1804 The Lewis and Clark Expedition reaches the Nebraska shore of the Missouri River.

1806 Explorer Zebulon M. Pike visits south-central Nebraska.

1819 The U.S. Army establishes Fort Atkinson.

1842–44 John C. Frémont leads an expedition through the Platte Valley and gives Nebraska its name.

1848 Fort Kearny is established to protect the hundreds of pioneers traveling west on the Oregon Trail.

1854 Congress creates Nebraska Territory through the Kansas-Nebraska Act.

1865 The Union Pacific Railroad begins building its line west from Omaha.

United States History

The United States is **1917–18**
involved in World War I.

The stock market crashes, **1929**
plunging the United States into
the Great Depression.

The United States **1941–45**
fights in World War II.
The United States becomes a **1945**
charter member of the U.N.

The United States **1951–53**
fights in the Korean War.
The U.S. Congress enacts a series of **1964**
groundbreaking civil rights laws.

The United States **1964–73**
engages in the Vietnam War.

The United States and other **1991**
nations fight the brief
Persian Gulf War against Iraq.

Nebraska State History

1867 Congress admits Nebraska as the
thirty-seventh state.

1917–18 Agriculture thrives in Nebraska as
farmers work to feed the nation during
wartime.

1921 Father Edward Joseph Flanagan
founds Boys Town on Overlook Farm
outside Omaha.

1934 Nebraskans vote to adopt a unicameral
legislature.

1939 Petroleum discovered in southeastern
Nebraska.

1944 The Pick-Sloan Missouri Basin Project
authorized to create dams, reservoirs,
and hydroelectric plants.

1960–64 Nebraskans approve constitutional amendments to strengthen state
government.

1982 Nebraska prohibits corporations from
buying farms or ranches in the state.

1986 Nebraska's gubernatorial race is the
first in U.S. history in which both major
candidates are women. Republican Kay
Orr becomes the first Republican
woman governor in U.S. history.

1992 Nebraska voters approve a state
lottery.

Fast Facts

The state capitol in
Lincoln

Statehood date	March 1, 1867; the 37th state
Origin of state name	From the Oto Indian word meaning "broad water" or "flat river," describing the Platte River
State capital	Lincoln
State nickname	Cornhusker State
State motto	Equality Before the Law
State bird	Western meadowlark
State flower	Goldenrod
State insect	Honeybee
State gem	Blue agate
State rock	Prairie agate
State fossil	Mammoth
State song	"Beautiful Nebraska"
State tree	Cottonwood
State grass	Little bluestem

Western meadowlark

Cottonwood tree

Omaha

State mammal	White-tailed deer
State fair	Lincoln (late August–early September)
Total area; rank	77,359 sq. mi. (200,359 sq km), 16th
Land; rank	76,878 sq. mi. (199,114 sq km), 15th
Water; rank	481 sq. mi. (1,246 sq km), 39th
Inland water; **rank**	481 sq. mi. (1,246 sq km), 33rd
Geographic center	Custer, 10 miles (16 km) northwest of Broken Bow
Latitude and longitude	Nebraska is located approximately between 40° 00′ and 43° 00′ N and 95° 00′ and 104° 00′ W
Highest point	Panorama Point, Johnson Township, 5,424 feet (1,653 m)
Lowest point	480 feet (146 m), at the Missouri River
Largest city	Omaha
Number of counties	93
Longest river	Missouri River, 450 miles (724 km)
Population; rank	1,584,687 (1990 census); 36th
Density	20 persons per sq. mi. (8 per sq. km)
Population distribution	66% urban, 34% rural

**Ethnic distribution
(does not equal 100%)**

White	93.8%
African-American	3.64%
Hispanic	2.34%
Other	0.99%
Asian and Pacific Islanders	0.79%
Native American	0.79%

Picking strawberries

Record high temperature	118°F (48°C) at Minden on July 24, 1936; at Hartington on July 17, 1936; and at Geneva on July 15, 1934
Record low temperature	–47°F (–44°C) at Camp Clarke, near Northport, on February 12, 1899
Average July temperature	76°F (24°C)
Average January temperature	23°F (-5°C)
Average yearly precipitation	12 inches (30.5 cm)

Nebraska's Natural Areas

National Recreational River

Missouri National Recreational River protects two stretches of the Missouri River in Nebraska.

National Scenic River

Niobrara National Scenic River flows between two distinct ecosystems: western grasslands and eastern woodlands.

National Forests

Nebraska National Forest in Blaine, Dawes, Sioux, and Thomas Counties is the largest hand-planted forest in the United States.

McKelvie National Forest is in Cherry County.

National Monuments

Agate Fossil Beds National Monument is renowned for its mammal fossils from the Miocene epoch.

Grasslands

Scotts Bluff National Monument

Homestead National Monument is the site of one of the first homestead claims under the Homestead Act of 1862 and a memorial to the pioneers who traveled west.

Scotts Bluff National Monument marks a promontory on the Oregon Trail.

State Parks

Nebraska has ninety-five state parks and recreation areas. *Fort Kearny* protected travelers heading west on the Oregon Trail. *Arbor Lodge* is J. Sterling Morton's elegant mansion. *Buffalo Bill's Ranch* was William Frederick Cody's home for more than thirty years.

Sports Teams

NCAA Teams (Division 1)
Creighton University Bluejays
University of Nebraska Cornhuskers

Cultural Institutions

Libraries
The Nebraska State Library (Lincoln) is the oldest library in the state and primarily a law library.

The University of Nebraska at Lincoln has the state's largest library collection.

Museums
The Joslyn Art Museum (Omaha) has a noted collection of Western art in addition to collections comprising ancient to modern art.

The Sheldon Memorial Art Gallery at the University of Nebraska (Lincoln) houses modern American paintings and sculpture.

The Cornhuskers

University of Nebraska

The University of Nebraska State Museum (Lincoln) has one of the world's largest mammoth fossil collections.

Performing Arts

Nebraska has one major symphony orchestra, one major opera company, and one major dance company.

Universities and Colleges

In the mid-1990s, Nebraska had sixteen public and more than twenty private institutions of higher learning.

Annual Events

January–March

Sandhill Crane Migration in Grand Island, Hastings, and Kearney (March)

St. Patrick's Day Celebration in O'Neill (March)

Sandhill crane

April–June

Arbor Day, statewide (April)

Willa Cather Spring Conference in Red Cloud (May)

Cinco de Mayo Festival in Scottsbluff (May)

Santee Sioux Powwow in Santee (June)

Grundlovs Fest, or Danish Day, in Dannebrog (June)

Swedish Festivals in Oakland and Stromsburg (June)

North Platte Nightly Rodeo (June–July)

July–September

Old Mill Days in Neligh (July)

Oregon Trail Days in Gering (July)

State Fourth of July Celebration in Seward (July)

Fur Trade Days in Chadron (July)

Winnebago Powwow

Wayne Chicken Show (July)

Winnebago Powwow (July)

Nebraska's Big Rodeo in Burwell (July)

Czech Festival in Wilbur (August)

Omaha Powwow in Macy (August)

John C. Frémont Days in Fremont (August)

Nebraska State Fair at Lincoln (late August–early September)

Rodeo and Stock Show in Omaha (September)

Husker Harvest Days in Grand Island (September)

Cowboy Poetry Gathering in Valentine (September)

River City Roundup in Omaha (September)

October–December

Ak-Sar-Ben Festival in Omaha (October)

Oktoberfest in Sidney (October)

Danish Christmas Festival in Dannebrog (December)

Light of the World Pageant in Minden (December)

Star City Holiday Weekend in Lincoln (December)

Nebraska's Big Rodeo

Famous People

Grace Abbott (1873–1939)	Social reformer
Bess Streeter Aldrich (1881–1954)	Author
Fred Astaire (1899–1987)	Dancer and actor
Max Baer (1909–1959)	World heavyweight champion boxer
Bill Baird (1904–1987)	Puppeteer
Howard Malcolm Baldridge Jr. (1922–1987)	U.S. secretary of commerce

Marlon Brando

George Beadle (1903–1989)	Nobel Prize-winning biologist
Marlon Brando (1924–)	Actor
William Jennings Bryan (1860–1925)	Politician and orator
Warren Buffett (1930–)	Investor and business executive
Johnny Carson (1925–)	Entertainer
Willa Cather (1873–1947)	Writer
Dick Cavett (1936–)	Entertainer
Richard B. Cheney (1941–)	U.S. secretary of defense
Montgomery Clift (1920–1966)	Actor
Crazy Horse (1842–1877)	Oglala Sioux leader
Edward Creighton (1820–1874)	Telegraph pioneer and banker
Sandy Dennis (1937–1992)	Actor
Mignon Good Eberhart (1899–1996)	Novelist
Val L. Fitch (1923–)	Nobel Prize-winning physicist
Edward J. Flanagan (1886–1948)	Priest and founder of Boys Town
Henry Fonda (1905–1982)	Actor
Gerald Rudolph Ford (1913–)	U.S. president
Robert (Bob) Louis Gibson (1934–)	Baseball player
Joyce Clyde Hall (1891–1982)	Founder of Hallmark Cards
Howard Hanson (1896–1981)	Composer and conductor
Gilbert M. Hitchcock (1859–1934)	Founder of *Omaha World-Herald*

Henry Fonda

J. Sterling Morton

Lawrence Klein (1920–)	Nobel Prize-winning economist
Swoozie Kurtz (1944–)	Actor
Harold Lloyd (1893–1971)	Actor and producer
Malcolm X (1925–1965)	Civil rights leader and reformer
Wright Morris (1910–1998)	Author
J. Sterling Morton (1832–1903)	U.S. secretary of agriculture and father of Arbor Day
John Gneisenau Neihardt (1881–1973)	Nebraska poet laureate
Nick Nolte (1940–)	Actor
George W. Norris (1861–1944)	Statesman
John J. Pershing (1860–1949)	Military leader
Susan LaFlesche Picotte (1865–1915)	Physician and social reformer
Red Cloud (1822–1909)	Oglala Sioux leader
Mari Sandoz (1896–1966)	Novelist and historian
Gale Sayers (1943–)	Professional football player
William Sessions (1930–)	FBI director
Standing Bear (1829–1908)	Ponca leader
Susette LaFlesche Tibbles (1842–1877)	Social reformer
Irene Worth (1916–)	Actor
Darryl F. Zanuck (1902–1979)	Motion-picture producer and movie-studio executive

To Find Out More

History

- Fradin, Dennis Brindell. *Nebraska.* Chicago: Childrens Press, 1995.
- Porter, A. P. *Nebraska.* Minneapolis: Lerner, 1991
- Thompson, Kathleen. *Nebraska.* Austin, Tex.: Raintree/Steck-Vaughn, 1996.
- Wills Charles, A. *A Historical Album of Nebraska.* Brookfield, Conn.: Millbrook, 1995.

Fiction

- Miller, Robert H., and Nneka Bennett (illustrator). *A Pony for Jeremiah.* Englewood Cliffs, N.J.: Silver Burdett, 1996.
- Ruckman, Ivy. *In Care of Cassie Tucker.* New York: Delacorte, 1998.
- Ruckman, Ivy. *Night of the Twisters.* New York: Harper-Crest, 1987.

Biographies

- Ferris, Jeri. *Native American Doctor: The Story of Susan LaFlesche Picotte.* Minneapolis: Carolrhoda Books, 1991.
- Robinson, Nancy. *Buffalo Bill.* New York: Franklin Watts, 1991.
- Streissguth, Tom, and Karen Ritz (illustrator). *Writer of the Plains: A Story About Willa Cather.* Minneapolis: Carolrhoda Books, 1997.

Websites

- **Nebraska Tourism Office**
  http://www.ded.state.ne.us/
  tourism.html
  Detailed site with complete
  information on travel and
  tourism in Nebraska

- **Nebraska State Website**
  http://www.state.ne.us/
  Complete information about
  Nebraska, its people, its history, and its government

- **Genuine Nebraska**
  http://www.visitnebraska.org/
  Travel and tourism pages as
  well as links to other
  Nebraska information

Addresses

- **Nebraska Tourism Office**
  P.O. Box 94666
  Lincoln, NE 68509-4666
  (800) 228-4307, ext. 754
  E-mail: tourism@ded2.ded.
  state.ne.us
  For travel and tourism infor-
  mation about Nebraska

- **Office of the Governor**
  Executive Suite
  Lincoln, NE 68509-4848
  For information about the
  history and government of
  Nebraska

Index

Page numbers in *italics* indicate illustrations.

Meet the Author

Sylvia McNair was born in Korea and believes she inherited a love of travel from her missionary parents. She grew up in Vermont. After graduating from Oberlin College, she held a variety of jobs, married, had four children, and settled in the Chicago area. She now lives in Evanston, Illinois. She is the author of several travel guides and more than a dozen books for young people published by Children's Press.

"The first step to writing any book is to read. I always head for my local libraries, and consult several encyclopedias and other reference books. Then I look for other books of fiction or nonfiction that are related to the history, geography, or people of the place

I'm working on. I use my computer to search for information on the Internet.

"If I'm working on a book about a state, I make a trip to the capital of that state as soon as possible. Usually I find a great deal of good information in the state library that isn't eas-

ily available anywhere else. Then I arrange to borrow some of the materials through the interlibrary loan service. Then I look in that city's bookstores, and I usually end up buying several books for my personal library.

"Last (although I've been working on it all along) comes the writing part. I sit at my computer for several hours each day. I use up reams of paper as I print out many drafts before I'm satisfied with the result.

"I learn so much while reading and writing, and there's nothing any more fascinating than learning more about my own land."

McNair has traveled in all fifty states and more than forty other countries.

Photo Credits

Photographs ©:

AP/Wide World Photos: 39, 40, 44 right, 111, 119 bottom, 122, 123 right, 123 center, 134 bottom
Corbis-Bettmann: 121, 134 top (MacFadden), 42, 85, 119 top, 120 (UPI), 14, 36, 123 left
Dembinsky Photo Assoc.: 60, 132 bottom (Claudia Adams), 59 (Mike Barlow), 58 (Darryl R. Beers), 6 bottom, 61 top (Dominique Braud), 91 (Gary Meszaros), 7 bottom, 90 left, 128 bottom (Rod Planck), 61 bottom (Carl R. Sams II), 92 (Bob Sisk), 108 bottom (Dusan Smetana)
Envision: 95 (Steven Needham)
Greater Omaha Convention Visitors Bureau: 117
Homestead National Monument of America, Beatrice, Nebraska: 26
Joel Sartore: 87, 112, 115, 131 bottom
Michael Forsberg: 6 center, 7 center, 50, 56, 71, 72, 77, 78, 108 top, 109, 113
Michael Malone: 97
Mike Malone & St. Joseph Hospital: 44 left
Nebraska Capitol Archives: 88
Nebraska Department of Economic Development: 90 right, 96 top, 125, 129 top
Nebraska State Historical Society: 32, 69
Nebraska State National Historical Society: 57, 135

NEBRASKAland Magazine, Nebraska Game and Parks Commission photo: 116, 118, 133 bottom, 17, 52, 54
North Wind Picture Archives: 9, 12, 16, 18, 20, 21, 23, 25, 28, 29, 34
Omaha Public Library: 110
P. Michael Whye: 45, 74, 80, 84, 86, 96 bottom, 98, 105, 114, 128 top, 130 top
Root Resources: back cover (James Blank)
Scotts Bluff National Monument: 22
Sitel Corporation: 99
Stock Montage, Inc.: 13, 30, 35
Tom Dietrich: 6 left, 38, 41, 46, 47, 73, 93
Tom Slocum/University of Nebraska Photography: 67, 132 top
Tom Till: 2, 8, 51 bottom, 130, bottom, 131 top
Tony Stone Images: 66 (James Blank), 7 left, 51 top (Tom Dietrich), 55 (Charles Doswell III), 107 (Kevin Horan), 6 right, 62, 129 bottom (Donovan Reese), 76 (G. Ryan & S. Beyer), 103 (Tom Tracy), cover (Larry Ulrich)
Unicorn Stock Photos: 81 (Bob Barrett), 65 (Cheryl R. Richter), 68, 124 (Jim Shippee)
University of Nebraska Archive Department: 31
Winnebago Indian News: 7, 102, 133 top
World-Herald Photo: 100 (Omaha World-Herald)
Maps by XNR Productions, Inc.